Willing to Yield

James 3:17

Jay W West

2013

"But the wisdom that is from above
is first … willing to yield…."
James 3:17

"If you are willing and obedient,
you shall eat the good of the land."
Isaiah 1:19

"But seek first the kingdom of God
and His righteousness, and all these
things shall be added to you."
Matthew 6:33

"Many applaud the one who seeks
first the kingdom but criticize the one
for whom all things are added."
*Pastor Bill Johnson,
Bethel Church, Redding, California*

WILLING TO YIELD

Pastor Jay W. West

Copyright © 2013 by Jay W. West

Anointed 2 Go MdM
Bellevue, NE

All rights reserved. This book is protected by the copyright laws of the United States of America. This book or any parts therein may not be reproduced, distributed, copied or transmitted in any form, not electronic, mechanical or any other means, or stored in a database or retrieval system without the prior written permission of the publisher. The use of short quotations or occasional passage copying for personal or group study is permitted and encouraged.

Unless otherwise identified, all Scripture quotations are from the New King James Version. Copyright © 1982 by Thomas Nelson, Inc. Used by permission. All rights reserved.

Scripture quotations marked (AMP) or "The Amplified Bible" are taken from THE AMPLIFIED BIBLE. Old Testament copyright © 1965, 1987 by The Zondervan Corporation. The Amplified New Testament copyright © 1958, 1987 by The Lockman Foundation. Used by permission.

Scripture quotations marked (MSG) or "The Message Bible" are taken from THE MESSAGE. Copyright © 1993, 1994, 1995, 1996, 2000, 2001, 2002. Used by permission of NavPress Publishing Group.

Scripture quotations marked (NIV) or "New International Version" are taken from the HOLY BIBLE, NEW INTERNATIONAL VERSION®. Copyright 1973, 1978, 1984 by International Bible Society. Used by permission of Zondervan. All rights reserved.

Scripture quotations marked (NLT) or "New Living Translation" are taken from the *Holy Bible*, New Living Translation, copyright © 1996. Used by permission of Tyndale House Publishers, Inc., Wheaton, Illinois 60189. All rights reserved.

Scripture quotations marked (TLB) or "The Living Bible" are taken from The Living Bible by Kenneth N. Taylor. Wheaton: Tyndale House, copyright © 1997, 1971 by Tyndale House Publishers, Inc. Used by permission. All rights reserved.

Scripture quotations marked (VOICE) or "The Voice" are taken from *The Voice Bible* Copyright © 2012 Thomas Nelson, Inc. The Voice™ translation © 2012 Ecclesia Bible Society.

ISBN: 978-0-578-12801-6

For further information, to contact Jay West for speaking, or to order resources:

Please email anointed2go@cox.net or go to http://www.anointed2go.com.

Contents

Opening Prayer 7
Dedications 9
Acknowledgments 13
Foreword 17
Introduction 19
Chapter One: Discovering the Power 23
Chapter Two: Study Time: Part 1 33
Chapter Three: Strange Prayers, Strange Answers 43
Chapter Four: Study Time: Part 2 55
Chapter Five: Being Uncommon 65
Chapter Six: Tolerated, Appreciated, Celebrated 81
Chapter Seven: Study Time: Part 3 93
Chapter Eight: Outmaneuvering the Manure 107
Chapter Nine: Perversion to Pastor 117
Chapter Ten: Flag Men Ahead 131
Chapter Eleven: Study Time: Part 4 143
Chapter Twelve: Taking Courage 155
Chapter Thirteen: There Goes One 171
Chapter Fourteen: Getting Un-Tongue Tied 181
Chapter Fifteen: Study Time: Part 5 199
Chapter Sixteen: Completing the Challenge Course .. 215
Epilogue 235
Notes 237

Opening Prayer

By Barbara Crider (Ministry Intercessor)

Dear Father,

I come before Your holy presence In the name of the Lord Jesus Christ Your Son. I thank You that You are God and above You there is no other. I pray for all people who hold this book in their hands that you would tune in their eyes to see, minds to understand, and hearts to know Your truth revealed in these pages. May they walk in a greater yieldedness in their lives as they relinquish their rights to You. May You also bless them with a bountiful yield that comes from being Your child. I praise You for the freedom that comes to a heart yielded to the move of You, Holy Spirit. What unexplainable peace and joy awaits Your blessed ones.

We love You, dear sweet Jesus, and we trust Your truth. It is our deepest desire to be more like You tomorrow than we are today. What a grand journey each opportunity to challenge us is to go deeper and press harder for the prize of Your high calling. We stand ready in anticipation for what You will do in and through us as You take the lead. It is in the mighty name of Jesus we pray. Amen.

Dedications

Samuel Lee and Sid Smith

BOTH of these men have impacted my life with entirely different scopes of persuasion, yet each of them presented Jesus in specific ways that I acknowledge, admire, treasure, and cherish as being rich and valuable assets for all to glean and learn from.

These two came from radically diverse backgrounds, in the face of opposing cultures, and walked in totally opposite lifestyles. Yet they each cultivated, promoted, and activated similar heavenly concepts and precepts that offered no disrespect, which ultimately changed other people's lives forever. They were both the real deal, and my life is substantially better because of their spiritual eloquence and dedicated life-giving influence.

If what they gave to me were to be auctioned off to the highest bidder, there would not be enough money, currency, or gold in the whole world to purchase these precious commodities. These are truly two great men of God.

When we first began to attend Eagle's Nest Worship Center in Omaha, there was a greeter who was always so friendly, and he and I soon became good friends. His name was Samuel Lee, but later he affectionately became known as Brother Lee. We could always count on a warm handshake or hug, a great smile, and a goofy joke, but his concern and love was genuine for everyone with whom he came in contact.

He was a native Omaha resident, serving in the Navy before becoming an Omaha police officer, where he actually was the first Black motorcycle officer. On several occasions, he came over to our house to fellowship and join with our family in special gatherings.

At his request, Brother Lee and I began to meet on certain afternoons to share and talk about the Bible. Even though he was almost thirty years older than me, he had a hunger to know more about God. One time, I challenged him to look beyond just greeting people and actually to offer to pray for anyone who looked a little down or discouraged. He came in the next week so excited because he had actually put that into practice that previous week and wanted to share how he had prayed for someone and how thankful that person was that he took that initiative. He was very authentic with his prayers when he met with me during these discipleship times.

Brother Lee passed away on April 12, 2013. I miss him and will always remember his smile, his handshake, and the way he greeted me with the words, "Hello, Pastor. Where have you been traveling?" Brother Lee embodied yielding to God as well as to others that he met. His heartfelt smile, handshake, and friendly greeting would sincerely bless, honor, encourage, and bring cheer and joy to all he met.

At the conclusion of the funeral service, our praise team sang a song called "The Keeper of the Door"[1] that so depicts Brother Lee's life and service to the Lord. I have included the words for all to read:

> I'd rather be a keeper of the door
> To know the power of Your presence, Lord
> To be able to gain entrance right into Your holy presence
> I'd rather be a keeper of the door
>
> One thing I ask, and I will seek
> To drink the water from Your living well
> My heart and flesh cry out, oh, God
> To know You in the place Your glory dwells
>
> I would let the door swing wide, inviting everyone to enter in
> Shine the light; show the way

I am also dedicating this book to my wonderful, inspiring friend Sid Smith, but you will have to wait until chapter sixteen to read all of his accolades and to discover why Sid is worthy of this shared dedication. At that point, you will understand more fully why I selected Sid Smith as a part of this twofold dedication. But I will add that meeting Sid was one of those rare intersections in life when deep down you know that something significant just happened, and that the meeting of this person is going to change your autobiography. That is indeed what took place when I was introduced to Sid Smith.

Now, let's go to the field and begin the yield!

Acknowledgments

BELIEVE it or not, eight months ago, when I began the process of writing this book, my plans were for it to be a short, four chapter book that I could easily write, proof, and publish prior to Easter, but it turned into sixteen chapters that took me on a much longer journey. While the task was at times arduous, God enabled me to complete the job and finish this writing course with joy, anticipation, and a sincere desire to see this work truly make a difference in the lives of many believers, just like you.

So my first thank you is attributed to my Heavenly Father for inspiring me with the message; to Jesus for giving me strength, power, and authority to complete the book; and to the Holy Spirit for His anointing to communicate truth and advance the kingdom of God.

Thank you, Diane, my lovely, kind, patient, and merciful wife. Thank you for your encouragement on the plane back home in November 2012 when you challenged me to write, and then for your unending support and prayerful stimulation to make this accomplishment possible. Thanks too for the many meals and late night snacks shared with me at my computer, back rubs at my desk chair, and persistent confidence in me even when I was not sure I could ever finish. Thank you too for your wonderful foreword that will bless all who read it. You are the best wife I could ever have. I am so glad God had me bump into you by the coke machine in college.

Jason! Wow, what can I say? Words really aren't adequate to describe the amount of time and work that you put into the editing and formatting process to assist me in the production of this book. Countless times I saw you yield your own schedule to help me complete certain tasks. There is no way I could have completed this book without your help. Thank you so much! Your foreword was inspiring and honest in your appraisal of yielding. I can't wait to read your first book, *Who Will Ascend*, which is also being published this summer and is listed at the back on the products page. Thanks for being my book buddy and the kind of son that makes me proud.

To my pastor, Jim Hart, your messages always present a challenge to go beyond what I often think I am capable of doing. They encourage me to believe for more and to expect great and wonderful opportunities to happen, because as we work the Word, the Word will work for us. I hope you enjoy reading parts of your messages in various chapters in this book. Thanks for your contribution to my life as my pastor and also as my friend. Go, Holy Spirit!

Cynthia Pleskac: You created an amazing book design and cover. It is outstanding! It is anointed! It is creative and innovative! I believe this cover will draw many people to want to read the book. I am so glad I met you at your church. Thank you for the dedicated hours of artistic flair and a custom blueprint that make the book shine with excellence.

Professor Peterson: I know, you just want to be known as Gary, but you earned that second Master's degree and became the head of the Humanities and English Department at Grace University. Congratulations! You deserve that title. But I want to give you another title: Good Friend. Thank you my friend, for the jokes, laughter, fun, recommendations, prayers, and serious times in your editing contribution. So many of your suggestions have been implemented, which will bring a positive impact and influence to those who read this book. I am impressed!

Barbara Crider: Thank you for your anointed prayer at the beginning of this book, for being on my intercessory team, and most of all, for being a good friend that I can count on.

To so many friends who contributed portions of various chapters, thank you so much for adding depth, joy, and compelling kingdom stories that surely will assist the yielding process for everyone who reads them.

Thank you to the many financial donors who helped make the publishing of this book possible. I am praying that you receive a financial yield back for your kingdom donations and gifts. From those who wish to remain anonymous to the following friends, I thank you so very much for your generosity.

Karen Anders	Harris and Diane Balko
Teri Bloebaum	Jessica Brown
Marta S. Coll	Rev. Fred Duncanson
Rev. F C Farwell	Dr. David N. Glesne
Jemma Hart	Micah Hart

Acknowledgments

Albert and Pia Hugo
Sid and Grace Jones
Jani Lackey
Jeanne Morrison
Marc and Bernice Spector

Gina Johnsen
Dr. Neil Kanning
Rev. Dennis and Stephanie Mitchell
Sid and Cynthia Smith
Eric Stubbs

And finally, thanks to "you" for purchasing and reading this book. Without you I would have lots of books sitting on my shelves, collecting dust. So you too are making a difference and contributing to this kingdom process, and I am very grateful.

*Please note: This book has undergone three critical editing reviews, in which two different trained editors have thoroughly commented, critiqued, and corrected all the errors they could find. In addition to those reviews, I personally reexamined and inspected the book a fourth time for final polishing. However, despite our best efforts, we admit that catching every typo and every grammatical error is a very difficult, tedious, and time-consuming task to accomplish. We have done our best, but please be gracious if you still find an occasional lingering discrepancy. Thank you.

Foreword

By Diane West

WHEN Jay asked me if I would write the foreword to this book, my first response to him was, "Me? Really? Are you sure?" You see, I don't see myself as much of a writer, so when he asked me, I was surprised. Yet, given our relationship as husband and wife, it also didn't surprise me. I was honored to be asked but hesitant to do it. Nevertheless, I yielded to Jay's request, mostly out of my love for him and our relationship with each other. I believe Jay had more faith and confidence in me than I did. That's the same way it is with our Father in heaven. Sometimes, He asks us to do something that perhaps is not in an area that we consider being one of our strengths or in our comfort zone. Second Corinthians 12:9 says, "My power works best in your weakness" (NLT). We often think up reasons or excuses why we couldn't or shouldn't comply. Our response to God should be, "Yes, Lord, and help me where I am weak."

God's desire is that we listen to the Holy Spirit's promptings and then yield and obey Him willingly. We are the conduit through which God's power flows. God can and will use us to bring salvation, healing, financial provision, and solutions to circumstances and situations that may appear hopeless or impossible. Even when we have fears and reservations about what God is asking us to do, we ought to yield to Him because of the love relationship we have with Him. We can trust Him because we know He is always with us, helping us every step of the way.

In this book, you will find many personal testimonies about how Jay and other individuals were willing to yield to God's requests. Had they not yielded to the Lord and obeyed Him, the outcomes would have been dramatically different. As it turned out, many people were touched by God, healed, encouraged, and grew in their faith and trust in Him. They experienced God's love in a tangible way through a willing human vessel.

My challenge to you as you read this book is to listen to what the Holy Spirit may be prompting you to do. Will you give Him all the reasons and excuses why you can't or shouldn't do it, or will you yield to Him out of your love for Him and then see how His power working best in your weakness can transform precious lives for His glory?

By Jason West

I have a confession to make: I don't like to yield. Does anyone else agree with me? I mean, when I am driving, I can deal with a red, yellow, or green light because I know the anticipated outcome. I will either have to stop, slow down, or proceed. I can deal with a stop sign too, for I know that my turn to go will come quickly. But when I come to a yield sign, I just groan inside a bit because I see the cars crossing the road, and I know I will have to yield to them for an indefinite amount of time. When will it be my turn?

Unfortunately, I have found this to be true of my spiritual life too. I sometimes find it difficult to yield to what God is doing, mainly because I have no idea how long this yielding process will take. I much prefer God's simple, clear-cut directions of "stop," "go," or "slow down." Those things I can do. However, when He says, "Just yield for a bit," I have a hard time dealing with the waiting process. He never seems to ask me to yield when it is convenient for me. Why is that?

I would imagine that many who are reading this book are just like me. You would much prefer a quick, simple answer from God, rather than a longer, complicated process. Yet, God has so much to teach us, and I believe a step toward learning to yield to Him can be taken simply by reading this book. Prepare to be challenged and stretched as you read. My father has tackled some prominent issues among believers today and has enhanced them with personal stories from his own experience. It is quite possible that through your reading you will repeatedly sense the need to yield to God as He brings course corrections to your life. Do not fear this—embrace it. For God desires to enlarge our capacity to yield to what He is doing so that we can be ready to obey Him at a moment's notice and to do what He is telling us to do.

Are you ready? Let the journey begin.

INTRODUCTION

WHILE checking out at a local Target store, before credit card scanners were available for the customers to use, my cashier that morning took my card and was trying to scan it with no success. I volunteered to try it, so she handed my card back to me. I leaned over the counter, ran the card through the slot, and it immediately registered and began the transaction.

This lady, who was a middle-aged African American, smiled really big and said, "You must have the Midas touch."

I responded that I thought I did, and then added by saying, "No, I think I have the Target touch."

She smiled once again and said, "Yesssss!"

Then I took courage. It was said of Paul in Acts 28:15 that he took courage. Many people are constantly praying for courage, and I am okay with that, but there are times we must simply take the courage, respond, and act. So I took courage and proclaimed, "You know what, I think I have the God touch!"

To this, she responded, "I think you do have the God touch." When she said that, her hand came up for an obvious high five, so I raised my hand up to meet hers, and just after our hands met, she spun around in the aisle. Well, I did not want to be outdone, so I spun around in the aisle too. White guys may not be able to jump, but we can spin (LOL)! At this point, everyone standing behind me in our checkout line backed their carts out and went to another cashier.

But what ensued was that we then had a five-minute discussion about God, her church, and my church. We quoted Scripture verses to each other, and we just had a blast talking about the kingdom of God. As I was about to leave, she thanked me, stating that her morning had been tough and she was not looking forward to the rest of her day. But now after I had come through her line, God had cheered her up through our interaction and my transaction that led to an action point that God used to bless and encourage.

This book you are embarking on is about yielding to the work of God in your life and mine. It is about supernatural times and opportunities when God directly intervenes and does something spectacular. But it is also about normal times like this one in Target when the circumstances are pointing in a direction, that if acted upon with courage can create a fantastic environment for the Holy Spirit to minister and change lives.

In my first book, *Downloads from Heaven*, so many people commented that my teaching, stories, and sharing were as if I was in the room with them sharing dialog about my experiences with God. That is my goal with this book too. I am praying that you will experience God in new and challenging ways that will encourage you to look for avenues, doors, openings, and opportunities to yield to Him in ways that promote the kingdom of God wherever you find yourself.

Like my first book, this is a fun and easy read. There will be some teaching and biblical references too, as I want you to see that the Bible is also proclaiming what I am sharing, but it won't be very deep theologically. I once heard and memorized a phrase that a well-known Bible teacher stated, which goes like this: "It takes a good theologian to help you misunderstand the Bible." This statement is explained in greater detail in Chapter 16.

Now, I certainly appreciate good theology and look for it in others to whom I listen, whether in person, on Christian television or YouTube, etc., but I also value good theophany. *Theology* helps us understand God through His word, but *theophany* helps us to understand God through experience and His appearance. Wikipedia quotes, "Theophany, from the Ancient Greek (ἡ) θεοφ▢νεια (*theophaneia*, meaning 'appearance of God')... . The term *theophany* has acquired a specific usage for Christians and Jews with respect to the Bible: It refers to the manifestation of God to man; the sensible sign by which the presence of God is revealed."[2]

I often ask people, "Where did Jesus do His ministry, including the miraculous?" I get all sorts of answers, but if we boil it down, He did those things in His body. And He is still doing those things today in His body. What is His body? It is made up of all who have accepted Jesus Christ as their Savior and Lord. I am a part of His body, and I am appearing with Him daily with many other people, whether at home, church, or in the marketplace.

Introduction

I am His body in action, demonstrating His love and encouragement, or releasing His gifts to others as they experience God in His appearance. But I am also stressing good theology and study of the Word of God as a biblical verification of what He is doing.

Several years ago, a church in the greater Omaha area gave its Easter Celebration the provocative title "Jesus, Live and in Person." My God is alive today and is living in me and around me, and I have communication with Him, just like I do with any of the rest of my friends. I can talk to them, and they talk to me. I can talk to God and He talks to me. Jesus says in John 10:27 that His sheep know His voice, they hear Him, and they follow Him. We follow God by listening, responding, and yielding to His voice.

My beliefs in God must be worked out in my own life so that when the opportunity strikes, whether at Target, the mall, the post office, at church, or on an airplane, I will be ready and willing to yield to what God is doing. Jesus said in John 5:19 that He only did what the Father was doing. To me that is the *key* and is the founding premise of my book, *Downloads from Heaven*. I will share more about this later, but for now, let's pray.

Dear Jesus,

I want to know You. I want to know Your Word and have a good theological perspective. But simultaneously I want to have a good theophany perspective that includes experiencing You wherever You might be appearing. I know that You are "live and in person." I recognize that since You live in me, I carry You with me, and You may just want to make an appearance at any time, including while I am checking out at Target. I pray that I will take courage, listen, speak up as I hear You speaking, and then respond as I see You responding. I simply ask that You use me to advance Your kingdom this day. I anticipate that before I get done with this book, I too will have many testimonies to share with others of how You used me to touch and make a difference in the lives of others, while promoting the kingdom and doing life together. I thank You by speaking the name of Jesus. Amen!

CHAPTER ONE

DISCOVERING THE POWER

A few years ago in 2008, I was invited to be a presenter at the International Lutheran Renewal Conference at North Heights Lutheran Church in the Minneapolis area. This was a great honor, since this conference has been in existence for many years and thousands of people attend each year. At the time of the invitation, Paul Anderson was the primary leader of this ministry, and before him it was Larry Christiansen. Paul asked me to speak and to come up with a catchy title that might attract folks to experience the power and presence of the Holy Spirit.

My presentation title was, "Fresh Manna, Fresh Manifestation," and I was given about ninety minutes to share my topic. As I awoke the morning of the day of the presentation, I was praying in bed, and I received two downloads from heaven regarding ministry that would happen. The Lord spoke to me and said that at some point in the middle of the presentation, I would stop and pray for eye problems, specifically those who battle floaters, shooting stars, and spots in their eyes.

One of the surprises to me was that nearly 1000 people showed up for my session. That was incredible. My presentation was videoed on the giant screens to the side of me, and while I am tall at 6' 7", I was a giant on those screens for sure.

Anyway, when I offered this prayer for eyes in the middle of the presentation, over fifty people got healed of visual problems in less than three minutes. This is verified on the CD and that you can order from me on the products page in the back of this book. I simply prayed twice from the front, never laying hands on anyone or specifically naming or praying for any of the eye problems. Those who needed prayer just stood up across the worship center. I prayed two times, checking in-between the two prayers to see how people were doing.

Years later, I learned from Kris Kildosher, who works in the healing rooms at Bethel Church in Redding, California, that there is a miracle when you check. I had been doing this for years myself, but had not used the phrase "there is a miracle when you check." At the time, I would have people raise their hands if they were experiencing significant healing. Now I have since learned from Randy Clark and Global Awakening to have people wave their hands over their heads if they are experiencing healing of 75% or higher. This works well, as it builds faith and releases encouragement in the room for those still waiting to be touched by the Holy Spirit.

One lady who was a leader in her church later shared that as a teenager she had injured her eye in some way and that for over forty years there was a kind of diagonal zigzag shadow in her eye. As I prayed, this totally disappeared. Every time she saw me during the conference she would exclaim that it was still gone and that she could see great. This is amazing. I give God all of the praise and honor for these miracles and many others that you will read about. But if I had not yielded to those instructions, the outcome might have been significantly different, as Diane West wrote in her foreword. To stop in the middle of a presentation when prompted by God and to pray for these specific needs really stretched me that day too.

The second download that morning was that the Lord instructed me to have people come forward at the end of the presentation who had never experienced a personal touch from the Holy Spirit in prayer. I honestly felt like maybe thirty or forty people might come forward, but over three hundred people came forward. As you read the rest of this chapter, you will discover what happened through the experiences of a retired couple who came to the conference for the very first time. These two classically-trained musicians whose main diet of worship music consisted of 16th- and 17th-century Lutheran chorale tunes were about to encounter the kingdom of God in a whole new way. After you read their firsthand account as a precursor, I will later share more about this in Chapter 13.

Before I get to that story, let's discover what the word *yield* actually means. The definition of the word *yield* really has two distinct themes.

First, there is the idea of giving the right of way to another, or to be flexible, resilient and stretchy. Within those thoughts are more direct phrases of actual giving up and surrendering. There are several connotations that accompany this definition including relaxed, easy, gentle and mild.

Can you see the influence of the Holy Spirit and the fruit of the Spirit in those words? The Holy Spirit will prompt us just as I shared above about the healing of the eyes, and our response in yielding at the appointed time will surely make a difference in the lives of others and also release kingdom power and authority into the situation.

The second and often less-thought-of explanation or meaning of the word *yield* is that of a farming term used to describe the size, proportion, and harvesting of a certain crop. The *yield* then becomes a quality or commodity of the product itself. What is actually produced is often referred to as the "crop" or the *yield*.

Every farmer knows that the *yield* does not just consist of the harvest of the crop, but also must include seed to plant for the next year. I will share in Chapter 15 how important this seed is to bringing an even greater *yield*, but please understand that in order to walk in the fullness of the things of God and progress from strength to strength, faith to faith, and glory to glory, we must value the *yield*. The pictures on the front and back covers of this book reveal both concepts of yielding that I have now shared with you.

As I am writing this chapter, I am also having some discussion with a friend on Facebook, and she wrote the slang "duh." I countered with "<u>D</u>ivine <u>U</u>nction <u>H</u>ere." In a sense, that is what yielding is about. As we give the right of way to the Lord, He then brings a yield or harvest back to our lives, in a divine unction here with us now. Yet it is more than just for us, but rather to impart truth and expand the kingdom of God so that others can also experience Jesus in a significant, impactful, and personal way.

Now, let's get to that narrative from my friends Diane and Harris who attended the conference. Here is some background information about them that you will be interested in for sure, as it clarifies and verifies that these are seasoned folks with advanced degrees and wonderful talents who were literally touched by God in significant ways.

Diane graduated from the Cincinnati Conservatory of Music with a Masters Degree in Violin Performance and Chamber Music. She was hired to the faculty of the University of Wisconsin in Superior in 1966, where she taught violin, chamber music, music theory and ear-training, and conducted the University Orchestra. In addition to her teaching duties at UWS, she won the chair of Concertmaster of the Duluth-Superior Symphony—a position she held for thirty-seven years. (They've been told that it's a world record for a woman.)

Harris graduated from the University of Minnesota in Minneapolis with a Masters Degree in Choral-Vocal Music Education. After eleven years of public school teaching, he joined the faculty of UW-Superior, where he directed the choral program, gave voice lessons, and taught choral music methods and music fundamentals with methodology to classroom teachers. In addition, for a number of years he conducted the Duluth-Superior Symphony Chorus and Opera Chorus.

As you read the following chronicle of my two friends Harris and Diane, who were long-time traditional Lutherans, see if you can begin to identify the two *yielding* definitions in their report. The story is fun and humorous, written in their own style and way, and I am confident you will enjoy it. This verbal recital will then launch us into our study of what it means to be willing to yield to God and what the benefits are for those who actually respond in that realm and way. Now, here is Harris's account of their experience.

> Our lives have been changed. I was baptized, confirmed, and was a member of the Lutheran Church Missouri Synod all of my life. I have sung in or directed church choirs for sixty-five years. We attended church regularly because that is what we did. My wife Diane was baptized, received first communion, and was confirmed in the Catholic Church. She went to confession and attended church regularly because that is what they did. Then one day in August of 2008, we both received a touch of the Holy Spirit, and from that day, that moment, our lives were changed.
>
> The accompanying testimonies are some of the highlights of our journey. We are not special people. We share them with you because the

evangelists and pastors we've met along the way and who have become part of our lives told us to give our testimonies, not for ourselves, but for the sake of the Gospel and the Glory of God. In that spirit, we share them with you in the hope that you, like we, come to know that THERE IS MORE.

It all began in the summer of 2008 when I was in the process of downsizing. I was sorting through and arranging by subject matter a large number of paperback books I had collected over many decades. One particular paperback caught my eye and piqued my interest: *Healing* by Francis MacNutt, a former Roman Catholic priest. Francis was married to a Southern Baptist lady named Judith whom he had met in Jerusalem.

As I browsed through the book, I was astounded by his testimony of receiving a baptism in the Holy Spirit and a subsequent healing ministry. I called to Diane, who was working at the computer, to tell her of this amazing book. She said she would "Google" his name to see if he was still active in the ministry.

To our surprise and delight, we learned the MacNutts have a School of Healing Ministry in Jacksonville, Florida, and Judith was appearing as a guest speaker at a Lutheran Renewal Conference on the Holy Spirit at North Heights Lutheran Church in Arden Hills, Minnesota. We "Googled" the conference and learned that it was to be held Wednesday through Saturday, the first week in August. We enrolled with great anticipation, not knowing what to expect.

We arrived in Arden Hills late afternoon on Wednesday, checked into our motel, ate a light dinner, and arrived at North Heights Lutheran Church in time to register before the first session that evening.

As we walked into the 2000-seat sanctuary we were stunned at what we heard and saw: an incredibly loud rock band playing unknown-to-us praise songs for a packed house of worshippers who were standing with arms raised, singing at the tops of their voices. A number of worshippers were also running throughout the sanctuary waving banners, and a few were even dancing exuberantly before the altar of the Lord.

Stunned is an understatement! We collapsed on two vacant chairs at the very rear of the sanctuary, gawked in awe and disbelief, turned to each other and asked, "What in the world have we gotten ourselves into?" This is not for us: two classically-trained musicians whose main diet of worship music consists of 16th- and 17th-century Lutheran chorale tunes. After considerable discussion, we decided that since we had paid our nonrefundable registration fees and for our lunch tickets, we would stay to hear the speakers and witness their ministering.

Thursday morning the guest speaker was Jay West, a former Missouri-Synod Lutheran school principal and evangelist who worked a great deal with adults and young people. At the conclusion of his talk, Jay asked how many in the audience had never experienced the presence—"received a touch"—of the Holy Spirit. Several hundred people raised their hands (including us). He then invited all who would like to have that experience to come forward and line up along the front of the sanctuary.

Over three hundred people went forward—along the front, the side aisles, middle aisles, and along the back, actually spilling out into the foyer of this extraordinarily large worship center auditorium. I turned to Diane and asked in as skeptical of a tone of voice as I could muster, "Do you want to go forward?" Her immediate response was, "Sure!" So, forward we went, with attitudes probably as opposite as you could imagine, finding room along the right front of the sanctuary. Jay then arranged for a "catcher" to stand behind each person in the event one of the persons for whom prayer was offered would "fall in the Spirit."

Jay began by telling us not to pray but to close our eyes and just focus on Jesus. I was not even sure how to do that, so I closed my eyes and just kept repeating in my mind, "Jesus, Jesus, Jesus, Jesus, Jesus." We then heard Jay offer a simple prayer, inviting the Holy Spirit to make His presence known. It went something like this: "Come, Holy Spirit. Make your presence known to these your people who are hungry to experience you. Come, Holy Spirit, touch them with the power of Your love and light." The next thing I heard Jay say was, "There goes one." Someone had fallen in the powerful loving presence of the Holy Spirit. I squinted my eyes to take a peek. IT WAS DIANE!! She was on her back on the floor with her arms raised heavenward! As she tells it:

It was a very strange sensation: It seemed I fell because I couldn't stand. I fell backward as gently as a feather; I was hardly aware of my "catcher" guiding me to the floor. I lay on my back, arms extended heavenward, feeling nothing but inexpressible peace.

At one point I lowered my arms to my sides only to have them go right back heavenward. As time went on, I was aware of others who subsequently fell in the Spirit, laughing, weeping, or speaking in tongues, but was totally unaware of what transpired with Harris. He told me that I later lowered my arms to the floor in the shape of a cross and that my face glowed.

Others then began to fall in the Spirit. I was standing there thinking, "This is what I get for being so skeptical; I'm going to be the only one left standing! Jesus, help me!" Within a matter of seconds I felt an incredible heat in my chest and "something" being lifted out. Then the heat returned to the top of my head and descended slowly through my entire body to the very tip of my toes . . . and over I went! The little lady who was my "catcher" had no difficulty in guiding me gently to the floor. I lay there with arms raised toward heaven, immersed in total peace: truly, "the peace that passes all understanding." There are no other words. As I lay there, I too was completely aware of all that was going on in the sanctuary: some people who had fallen in the Spirit were laughing in the joy of the Lord, others were weeping, and others were speaking in tongues. After a several minutes I thought, "I really don't have to have my arms raised like this." I brought them down to my sides from where they immediately shot back up! That was a surprise; I was amazed! After some time, however, I did bring them to my sides. Big mistake!

As I lay quietly, eyes closed, soaking in this incredible experience, I suddenly felt a heavy pressure on my chest and the lower part of my face. I opened my eyes in alarm to see an enormous blue bottom settling down on me. The very large lady to my right had fallen in the Spirit and her little "catcher" couldn't handle her. She sat right on me! Immediately two men from the congregation rushed to lift her off of me and guide her to a seat in the auditorium where she began to laugh hysterically in the Spirit. The experience of peace left with that lady, so I decided to sit on the floor, give thanks to the Holy Spirit for experiencing His presence, and contemplate the "sitting": whether it was Satan's attempt to give lie to the experience or the Holy Spirit saying, "Harris, lighten up!" I concluded it was the Holy Spirit.

As I continued to sit, observing other manifestations and keeping watch over Diane, I could not help but notice the beatific expression of peace on her face. After several more minutes she slowly lowered her arms to the floor in the form of a cross. I thanked God for His unfathomable love, for Diane, and for this incredible experience. Several minutes later I helped Diane to her feet and we returned to our seats soaking in the presence and wonder of the Holy Spirit. I did stop by the "big lady" to ask her, "Did you sit on me?" to which she loudly squealed, "YES!" as she continued to laugh loudly in the joy of the Lord.

Another amazing aspect of this touch of the Holy Spirit was that for two or three weeks after we returned home, we just marinated in indescribable joy. When I went for my daily walk/jog, I could not keep from singing to myself. All of nature seemed so vibrantly alive, as did we. Diane commented on how vivid the colors were of sky and earth as she took her daily walks. Also, for both of us, how alive the Holy Scripture became: not mere words, but a living text that touched our hearts and minds. Glory to God!

Additionally, after two weeks—as I was walking—it came to my mind that I had not used the Albuterol inhaler for my asthma, that I had experienced no tightness in my bronchial area since the conference. I then knew that when I had experienced the incredible heat in my chest and "something" being lifted out, God had healed me of forty-five years of asthma! I was awestruck! I didn't know how to process that! Thank you, Jesus! Then the words of Isaiah 40:5 in the King James Version—the text of the first chorus of Handel's *Messiah*—came to mind, and has remained:

> *And the glory of the Lord shall be revealed,*
> *And all flesh shall see it together:*
> *For the mouth of the Lord hath spoken it.*

Journey

One of the foundational verses of this book is Isaiah 1:19, which says, "If you are willing and obedient, you shall eat the good of the land." As you read the testimony of Harris and Diane, can you identify a "good of the land" result? Can you recall a time when you yielded to God and you were surprised at how it all turned out? Write down that remembrance either here at the end of this chapter or in a journal. Then pray, asking God to help you to yield quicker and faster the next time He calls on you to do something. Anticipate the good of the land surprises in your life because God just loves to bless, encourage, and demonstrate His love toward you. Now say out loud, "I am on a new journey that requires me to yield to God."

Finally, what did you like best about the history and testimony of Harris and Diane and why? Write down your thoughts as a remembrance to how God worked in their lives so you can be encouraged that He will also work in your life too.

Chapter Two

Study Time: Part 1

LET me briefly remind you in a capsule form of the definitions of the word *yield*. One definition is to give the right of way to someone, to be flexible and resilient, including giving up and surrendering. Another definition of the word *yield* is a farming term used to describe the size of a crop. But I want to add one more definition in the mix, and that is "to do or to make." Say that out loud: "To do or to make."

Let's read the initial biblical text from James 3:13–18:

> Who is wise and understanding among you? Let him show by good conduct that his works are done in the meekness of wisdom. But if you have bitter envy and self-seeking in your hearts, do not boast and lie against the truth. This wisdom does not descend from above, but is earthly, sensual, demonic. For where envy and self-seeking exist, confusion and every evil thing are there. But the wisdom that is from above is first pure, then peaceable, gentle, willing to yield, full of mercy and good fruits, without partiality and without hypocrisy. Now the fruit of righteousness is sown in peace by those who make peace.

I am not going to spend a lot of time dissecting this section of Scripture, but I want you to see the context by which the phrase "willing to yield" is used. It is within the framework of wisdom and being wise. A person who yields is someone who uses wisdom in a confident yet meek way that promotes the kingdom of God without hypocrisy. Our goal is to be authentic Christians. Let me say it this way: Our goal is to be authentic believers in Jesus and followers of Jesus, without religious overtones. We definitely don't need more religion, but we do need more of Jesus. Would you agree?

Wisdom is often released and expressed in our vocal interchange of thoughts. We communicate our wisdom to others by how we respond to situations and circumstances. The Bible says that out of the abundance of the heart, the mouth speaks (Matthew 12:44). The Bible also says in 1 Corinthians 15:33 that evil company corrupts good habits. Let me illustrate this with the following story.

When I was in junior high, I started hanging around with a crowd of students who were cussing and swearing a lot, and so I started to do the same. These profane words were not a part of my previous vocabulary, but as I started to dabble with this new crowd, my language was perverted into a "down-word" spiral that included a growing lexicon of obscene language. In other words, my dabble changed my babble.

Farther up in James 3:10–12, we read the following:

Out of the same mouth proceed blessing and cursing. My brethren, these things ought not to be so. Does a spring send forth fresh water and bitter from the same opening? Can a fig tree, my brethren, bear olives, or a grapevine bear figs? Thus no spring yields both salt water and fresh.

So there I was in junior high, speaking so much ungodliness when at school, yet kind, considerate words when at home with my family. I was the perfect imperfect picture of someone who needed Jesus, and who needed to have his mouth washed out with soap. Those very words are used in the Message Bible at Hosea 2:17, in which God says that He will wash out our mouths with soap to get rid of all the dirty false God names.

Aren't these words from Malachi 3:2 appropriate? "But who can endure the day of His coming? And who can stand when He appears? For He is like a refiner's fire and like launderers' soap." The words from Titus 3:3–5 in the Message Bible are fantastic: "It wasn't so long ago that we ourselves were stupid and stubborn, dupes of sin, ordered every which way by our glands, going around with a chip on our shoulder, hated and hating back. But when God, our kind and loving Savior God, stepped in, he saved us from all that. It was all his doing; we had nothing to do with it. He gave us a good bath, and we came out of it new people, washed inside and out by the Holy Spirit."

This is exactly what I needed, as I was yielding to horrible language. Yet, within two years, while watching a Billy Graham television special, I knelt down and prayed, asking Jesus into my life to begin cleansing me from all of my past sins. And guess what? It was the fastest bath ever. I was clean! Wow! Let me say it backwards. Wow!

Back in James 3:18, after the section about being willing to yield, the passage says that "the fruit of righteousness is sown in peace, for those who make peace." I had just made peace with Jesus, and the fruit of new righteousness was being revealed in new vocabulary, replacing cursing with blessing. The peace that ensued was amazing, simply amazing. I was morphing into a new person, and one of the initial evidences was that my language was changing. It was a rapid change. I am grateful for a God who can make rapid changes, aren't you?

In John 4:14, Jesus offers these words, "The water that I give him will become in him a fountain of water, springing up into everlasting life." Then in John 7:37–38 Jesus says, "If anyone thirsts, let him come to Me and drink. He who believes in Me, as the Scripture has said, out of his heart will flow rivers of living water."

Fountains and rivers. Say these out loud:

Fountains!
And rivers!
Fountains!
And rivers!

God promises both to us. And both are important to our walk with Him. Let me explain. On our deck we have a fountain. In fact, we have two outside fountains. My fountains are for my individual use. I can turn them on when I want and enjoy them. I am able to control the spray and change it at will. These are entirely for my use and for those in my family. They are personal, practical, and fun.

However, I live about a mile from the Missouri River, and when I go to one of the parks near the river, I see people fishing, boating, sailing, skiing, or just walking along a path near the river. The river is for everyone's use, and only God can control it.

God says there are times in your life and mine when we just need some quiet fountain times. We need personal times of refreshing. I like how Acts

3:19–20 reads: "Repent and be converted so that your sins may be blotted out so that times of refreshing may come from the presence of the Lord, and that He may send Jesus …"

You and I both need times of personal refreshing that those relaxing fountain times can bring and establish in our lives. We just need that personal touch from Jesus to renew, refurbish, rejuvenate, and perhaps even revive us for the next step in our journey with Him.

But we also need those river times when we are interacting with others, sailing with Jesus, and providing an atmosphere for others to discover the Kingdom of God in their lives too. When we are engaged with the river, we are in the flow of what the Lord is doing, and He uses us to advance His purposes, plans, and procedures in helping others who may just be exploring the river to actually come into His presence and also enjoy times of personal refreshing. It is a neat deal, for sure.

In the past, we hosted Kingdom Encounters at our home on a regular basis. Our intentions were to assist, promote, and help others experience the flow of the river of God in a safe, yet challenging, environment. At Kingdom Encounters, personal growth was experienced, coupled with training in worship, prayer, teaching, and signs and wonders, including healing and other manifestations, to show what Jesus is like and how the Holy Spirit operates. People came from all over the city and even from cities two to three hours away to experience God and have an encounter with Him. It was amazing! I'll share more on this later.

Often when I teach this in person, I will have someone come up to the front and I will give that person a capped water bottle and ask him or her to shake some out on the floor. Some are initially timid, while others are much more demonstrative. It is a good example that gets the rest of the congregation involved, because after the person shakes out some of the water, I then ask the audience to tell me why the water came out of the bottle.

I get many answers, including, "he took the cap off" or "he was obedient to what I asked" or "he shook the bottle" or "he poured it out." While all of these are great answers, I often will ask the person to shake more water out again for everyone to watch closely. I then ask again why the water came out of the bottle, and I receive more similar answers, sometimes with someone actually getting the right answer.

Drum roll, please.

Study Time: Part 1

The reason the water came out of the bottle is because there was water in the bottle. Now, that may sound simplistic or even somewhat of a play on words, but my goal in every example, whether in person or written, is to drive a point home. Whatever is springing forth out of your life is already in you. If you are harboring anger, then anger will be released. If you are full of strife, then strife will certainly come out. If bitterness is on the inside, then bitterness will be on the outside too. Whatever you are yielding to will come out. If you yield to love, then love will appear. If cooperation, the others will enjoy your compatibleness. If obedience, you will experience the good of the land. And if you are full of the Holy Spirit, then you can expect signs and wonders to happen on a consistent basis, because whatever is in you will come out. Matthew 15:11 says that it is not what goes into the mouth that defiles a man, but what comes out. And Matthew 11:34 proclaims that out of the abundance of the heart, the mouth speaks.

In 1997, while driving home to Hugoton, Kansas, from Amarillo, Texas, which was our closest airport, I had a car accident. It had snowed lightly a couple of hours earlier, and as I was heading out of the small rural town of Stratford, Texas, I began to increase my speed. Suddenly, there were two sets of headlights coming directly toward me on that two-lane rural highway. Apparently, a semi truck pulled out to pass another truck and did not see me coming toward him. I immediately turned toward the shoulder of the right side of the road, hoping to avoid a collision. But my tires caught some of that recent snow packed on the side, and I began to spin wildly toward those trucks.

A scream came out of my mouth due to the sudden fright of the situation, and only one word was uttered. At the top of my lungs, I screamed the word "JESUS!" That one-word prayer was heard and answered as I slammed with great force into the front of the truck, then bounced off a parked car on the side of the road in that wilderness area, and spun one more time, ending up in a ditch twenty feet off the road, facing the opposite direction from which I was originally driving.

Had this accident occurred back when I was in junior high, there probably would have been a slew of curse words of various degrees and colors that would have proceeded from my mouth, but at this season in my life, what was in me came out. And His name was Jesus. Jesus was in me, so that is what was shouted.

I believe that people's lives will always go in the direction of their most dominant thoughts. Proverbs 23:7 says, "As a man thinks in his heart so is he," and Judges 8:21 says, "As a man is, so is his strength." As we combine those two passages, we discover that what we are thinking about determines our strength.

One of the things I think about a lot is how to bless and help others financially. Isaiah 32:8 says, "A generous man devises generous things, and by generosity he shall stand." I honestly love it when God prompts me to give something to someone else, because I know as I yield to God, that person is going to get blessed, and that is good theology; but I also know that as I give, I will get a return, and that is good theophany. I rely on God's word for the theology and on God's experience for the theophany. And when I get that return, it is always—and I literally mean always—better than what I gave away. As I yield and give or plant in the lives of others, my harvest comes in and my yield or size of the return is fantastic. Below are a couple of examples in which, as John Wimber used to say, God gets all of the credit, honor, and glory, but we get the hugs.

Years ago, when Diane and I were only married for perhaps five years and we were pretty new at hearing from God and yielding to His direction, I received a rather challenging command from the Lord. We were attending a worship conference out on a farm that was about twenty miles from our suburban church in the Houston area. We had a guest speaker who quoted from Acts where it says that the believers had all things in common, sold their possessions, and gave the money to those who had a need.

When he said that, I had an impression from God that we were to sell our car and give the money away to a family in our church that was struggling economically. The problem was that we only had one car, so this was a big challenge indeed. My wife and I prayed about it and we felt God was in it, so we asked some others to pray in agreement with us. We received lots of good prayer support, and our lead elder prayed that the car would sell for more than the appraised value. This conference was on a Saturday, and by Monday I heard from a friend about a Christian used car salesman. Now, I know this sounds like an oxymoron, but it was the truth.

So on Tuesday I called this man. His name was Robert, and he had a small lot consisting of probably forty cars or so. I went over to him and

Study Time: Part 1

shared with him what I thought the Lord had told us, and he proceeded to have our car appraised.

You have to understand that this was an older AMC Spirit. It had a very bad gray oxidized paint job, and the whole car would often shake when I drove it. I often prayed when I drove this car, and that way I was praying in the Spirit (LOL). I knew the car was not worth much with so many miles on the odometer, but I still thought it was worth more than what these appraisals came in at, which was $250. This was a disappointment for sure.

Robert could see that I was disappointed, and being the wise car salesman that he was, he made a suggestion. He encouraged me to bring the car back the next day because he had another appraiser who was out of town but would be returning. This man was usually more generous with appraisals, so that was our new plan.

The next day my phone rang, and it was Robert telling me he had a buyer for my car. I responded, "That's great! Go ahead and sell it to that person." But Robert said that if he sold it he would have to charge the commission, but if I sold it he would not charge me the commission. Now let me ask you, when was the last time you heard of a car salesman who gave up his commission?

So I took it over to this man, and he walked around it a couple of times and literally kicked all four of the tires, and then he looked at me and said, "I will give you $600 for the car." This was amazing. The car actually sold in less than twenty-four hours from the time I contacted Robert, without any for-sale sign or marketing, and it sold for more than the appraised value as our lead elder had prayed. Then Robert did all of the paperwork for free too. God was working big-time on our behalf, but now I had another problem in that I did not have a car to get home from Robert's dealership, which was at least fifteen miles away from home. But God came through again.

Robert had a beautiful cream colored two-door Buick in cream puff condition with a landau roof, power windows, and many options that my AMC did not have. Robert told me that he reserved this car for missionaries who would come home from the field, and that we could drive it for as long as we needed for free. Wow, a free car! This is spectacular, amazing, and phenomenal.

So Diane and I had a nice car to drive and $600 in our pockets, so we decided to go out to eat to celebrate, and we selected a restaurant in the

Houston area that we enjoyed at that time called The Black Eyed Pea. It was a southern franchise with great food. The night we went there, it was packed with a long waiting line, but we decided to stay. We were finally seated and proceeded to order our food. When our order arrived, I prayed a simple prayer, asking God to confirm that we were still to give the $600 away, as this was all new to us and a very big step of faith.

After our meal, our wait staff came by and offered to bring us anything else we may want, but we said no, we just wanted our bill for the evening. I will never forget it, but the waiter said, "There is no bill." I inquired as to how this could be possible, and he said that someone else in the restaurant had paid our bill. So we quickly looked around and did not see anyone we recognized, but as we glanced toward the door, it appeared that Diane's orthodontist was just leaving. So we thanked the waiter and then left.

The next day, I called that doctor and started by stating that I wanted to ask a couple of strange questions. I first asked if he had been at the same restaurant the night before, and he said yes, he had, to which I followed up by asking if he had by chance paid our bill, and he further stated that yes, he had done that as well.

I then asked why he did that for us, and all he could say was that he saw us pray before our meal and at that exact moment felt prompted to purchase our meal. You may remember that during that prayer I asked God to confirm that we were to give the full amount of the money away. So we took that as our confirmation and that evening, we took the full $600 over to the family that was struggling financially.

What happened? We yielded to God, and He provided a larger yield back to us. During those nine years at that church, I think we owned fifteen cars, all paid cash. We met a new friend who would take me to the car auction, and I would buy a car at a very low price, keep it six months or less, and then sell it to someone else for a higher price than I paid for it, and we just kept doing this for a number of years. We have been blessed with cars for many years, and the pattern continues to this day. I have so many car stories, that I could write a small book just on that subject, because that was not the only car we gave away and I just know it won't be the last. Isn't God amazing? I will continue more on this study time as we progress through the book, but it is time for a little drink from the fountain and a river raft journey.

Journey

Do you know the difference between a river and a swamp? The primary distinction is flow. A swamp does not have any flow to it, so it is not able to sustain much life. But the river flows within its banks and life is the profuse evidence of the river, coupled with the intensity or measure of the flow. In John 3:34 we are told that the Spirit is given without measure. And many places in the Bible refer to the river of God. God is moving and flowing, and He really wants us to flow with Him in obedience to the direction He is going.

Have you ever felt like you were paddling upstream against the current of the Lord? What was it that prompted you to go against the flow? How did it conclude? Was it a profitable experience? Often the things God tells us make no sense to the natural mind, and the Bible even speaks to this, but if we will yield to His voice, I believe we will always experience a wonderful yield in return. Can you trust God today with the things He is asking you to do, even if they stretch you or make no sense at all? Giving a car away when we only had one car made no sense, yet God was in it and had an answer. He had a ram in the thicket for Abraham and he had a car on the lot for me. Abraham did not see the ram, and I didn't see the car, but God saw both and knew that faithfulness would produce a Godly harvest.

First Corinthians 4:2 says that the requirement of stewards is faithfulness, and we are stewards of the kingdom of God on earth today. How will you respond the next time He asks you to do something out of your comfort zone? What will your answer be?

Take some time right now to jot down some of the thoughts and feelings you have after reading this chapter. Pen those thoughts here on the pages of this book or in a journal where you can access them later. Then, just pray to the Lord about these thoughts and let Him know what you are thinking. I have a suspicion that if you are honest and yield your life to Him now in these areas, that you will be in for a big surprise in the near future. Commodities in the stock market referring to yields are often called futures. You are going to be so amazed at what God does with your future as you yield to Him. I can't wait to hear and learn of your testimonies too. The Epilogue will advise you of how to communicate your testimonies with me.

Chapter Three

Strange Prayers, Strange Answers

Selected Verses in the Message Bible:

Listen, God! Please, pay attention!
Can you make sense of these ramblings, my groans and cries?
King-God, I need your help. Every morning you'll hear me at it again.
Every morning I lay out the pieces of my life on your altar and watch for fire to descend.

HAVE you ever prayed anything like that prayer above from Psalm 5:1–3? On many occasions as I wake up in the morning, I often launch right into my list too. I am not as presumptuous to declare, "Listen, God," but with my attitude, I might as well be.

A number of years ago, that is exactly what happened. I woke up and started praying my list, and God interrupted me, saying, "You did not even say 'good morning' yet." I stopped short and half-heartedly apologized. Then He asked me if I was interested in what He was doing while I was sleeping, because the Bible says that God never sleeps. Thus, while we are sleeping in our part of the world, God is awake on the other side of the world, listening and communicating with many others like me who are praying all at the same time.

The Lord actually told me once that He could talk to 1,000 different people in 1,000 different languages at the same time. In reality, I believe the number is much higher, but 1,000 is a manageable number, yet still hard for me to understand. I know a little Spanish, and I can speak some words very slowly, but I have to translate in my mind, conjugate the verbs, and think really hard about what I am saying in Spanish while also thinking about it in English. God is so amazing that, while we are sleeping, He is talking to many people in other parts of the rest of the world who are not sleeping.

So God began to show me that I needed to be interested in what He is doing first, before I put my requests out on the table. Isn't that what "seek first the kingdom of God" is about, as presented in Matthew 6:33? So, this began a time of my awakening and then simply saying, "Good morning, Lord," waiting for His reply (which was always instantaneous) and then inquiring how things were going for Him. Sometimes, He told me things that made Him happy, and other times things that saddened Him. He actually told me some things that were direct answers to prayers others had prayed, and I would record some of those things and then read about the very testimonies a month or two later in various Christian periodicals. Now, that was fun, for sure.

What was happening? I simply yielded another area of my life to the Lord, and He began to bless and encourage me in the process, along with bringing a yield to my life as I would learn and see the value of this kind of prayer life that exalts Jesus and cares about His kingdom first. Then, like the model in the Lord's Prayer, I can bring my petitions to the Lord in a quality way that blends my relationship with Him and His Kingship in my life. What a joy it is to pray in this manner.

Psalm 17:15 in the Message Bible concludes this way: "And me? I plan on looking you full in the face. When I get up, I'll see your full stature and live heaven on earth." I like what Psalm 24:7 and 9 read. Both verses say the same thing, as if to challenge us to do what God would like us to do. "Wake up, you sleepyhead city! Wake up, you sleepyhead people! King-Glory is ready to enter."

Now, follow that with these words from Proverbs 20:13 (MSG): "Don't be too fond of sleep; you'll end up in the poorhouse. Wake up and get up; then there'll be food on the table."

Finally, look at these words from Psalm 5:11–12 (MSG): "But you'll welcome us with open arms when we run for cover to you. Let the party last all night! Stand guard over our celebration. You are famous, GOD, for welcoming God-seekers, for decking us out in delight."

I really like that part about God being famous for welcoming God-seekers, because in that realm, God's answers may not make any sense to us, but to God they are the right answers at the right moments at the right locations for the right people. If the folks who are getting the answers will yield to them, they will see amazing results, miracles, and signs and wonders that will bless everyone involved.

Let me give you an example. Years ago, I was ministering at Christ the King Church in the Columbus, Ohio, area, and during prayer ministry after my message, I apparently gave some unusual instructions to a lady who was having back pain. I went back to that church a few months later and this particular lady approached me, asking if I could remember her. I had to respond that I could not.

She stated that was okay, since I meet thousands of people every year while traveling and ministering at so many different churches. She told me that I had prayed for her chronic back pain, and then told her to go eat some bananas. Admittedly, this sounds strange, but read on. When she went home, her children kept encouraging her to eat some bananas, but they did not have any in the house, so she finally went to the grocery store, purchased two bananas (since I had given the plural version of the word), took them out to her car, peeled them, and ate both of them.

Immediately, her back pain disappeared, and what she had experienced for many years was completely gone. She had full mobility in her back, could bend forward, backward, and sideways, and had no pain walking, sitting, or sleeping. She asked me what I thought about all of that, and I simply stated that I was obedient to share the word with her and she was obedient to respond to it. As a result, she was healed. I took her to Isaiah 1:19, which is on the title page of this book, and showed her that she had received the good of the land by yielding to the "NOW" word of God for her at that very moment.

Think of it. Isn't this amazing? This lady got well and her back healed through prayer, but also through a command of God to actually take a step of faith. In the process, God honored her faith that she yielded to God, even though it sounded ridiculous.

Let's shift gears and look at another strange answer to prayer, or so it would seem. Psalm 135:5 (MSG) says, "I, too, give witness to the greatness of God, our Lord, high above all other gods. He does just as he pleases—however, wherever, whenever. He makes the weather—clouds and thunder, lightning and rain, wind pouring out of the north."

I am a firm believer in the Bible and what it says. Back in the early 1990s I did a study of the weather and looked up over 150 verses on all sorts of weather-related issues in the Bible and could not find any Scriptures or references that gave any credit to the devil for the weather, but rather gave them all to God. The reason I did this study was because I often hear Christians blaming or praying against the devil regarding harsh weather, but giving God the glory and credit if it was a bright sunny day, or perhaps raining after a season of drought. Yet I knew both arguments could not be correct.

Now, fast forward to 2009, around Thanksgiving when many of the football bowl games are announced for that season. We live in Nebraska, and the Cornhuskers had been invited to play in the Holiday Bowl in San Diego, California, which was my hometown area. So I thought it would be cool if we could go to the game as a family. After all, I had plenty of airline miles to get us there for free, plus I knew how to navigate the city. My brother has a condo on the beach that he often rents to us, so it would be a perfect vacation to go and watch the thirty-first Holiday Bowl.

I shared the idea with my family, and they were delighted. Then I decided to pray and ask God if it was okay with Him, and every time I prayed, I heard that it was going to rain. Now this is approximately five weeks in advance of the game, and while the weather forecasters are pretty good at what they do, I don't know of anyone who can forecast five weeks in advance. And while I enjoy watching football, I do not like to do it in the rain, especially if you have paid a bowl ticket price to get in, so we decided as a family that this was not a wise thing to do and elected not to proceed with our plans to attend the game.

We made the right decision because, while the Nebraska team won the game and the other team did not even score a point, there were many empty seats in the stadium because it rained for the first time in the thirty-one year history of the Holiday Bowl, and it rained hard too. We yielded our plans to God because He knew what was going to happen.

There had been previous times when I had been told by God what the weather was going to be, and He gave me permission to pray against that weather or to change it, but this time in San Diego that was not an option. I do appreciate that God told us in advance and led us not to attend the game.

God knows what is happening in the future and can download these things to us so easily like I identified in my first book.

Now, let me share a time when God had me pray to change the weather. I was invited to minister at a church way up in Sandpoint, Idaho, which is about thirty miles south of Canada. I had flown into Spokane, Washington, and my host drove me to Sandpoint. Sandpoint is a beautiful mountain town with a fantastic lake. I was there for a Friday through a Sunday for ministry, with my travel taking me home on Monday. I got there on Friday, and we had scheduled a meeting for that evening, so I had some time to kill. I turned on the television and learned from the Weather Channel and the local stations that Sandpoint was to get approximately fifteen inches of snow overnight and into Saturday. I am aware that people who live in the snow know how to navigate in it, but I also realize that fifteen inches could really put a damper on the meetings, if not cancel them altogether.

So I began to pray, and God would tell me when to pray and when to stop. He would tell me to rebuke the snow and to pray for the winds to blow in a different direction. Other times, He would simply say, "Don't pray right now," and then later instruct me to pray again. This went on all evening and into the night. Even when I was sleeping, He would wake me up and tell me to pray for this storm to move. So I yielded to His direction every time He instructed me.

The strangest thing happened. The next day, we woke to a bright sunny day, but no snow anywhere to be seen. The weather folks came on and kept exclaiming how amazed they were that it did not snow in Sandpoint. It had snowed all around that mountain community, but apparently not one flake fell in that town, and the weather people kept commenting on how amazed they were.

So, we had our meetings as planned on Saturday and then that evening, I inquired of the Lord as to what was going to happen on Sunday. He said it would snow one inch, but not to worry or pray about it at all as it would not disrupt anything or any part of our meetings. Well, sure enough on Sunday morning there was one inch of snow on the ground.

Then on Sunday evening as I was going to sleep and thanking the Lord for a marvelous weekend, He actually asked me what I wanted the weather to be on Monday for my departure. I asked that it would be partly sunny, and in the mid-thirties when my plane would take off so that no deicing would have to happen at the airport.

When we got up on Monday morning and were driving from Sandpoint, Idaho, to Spokane, Washington, the temperature started at seventeen degrees but gradually warmed as we made our way. Finally, when I was seated on the plane for takeoff, the pilot came on the speaker and announced to us that the temperature was in the mid-thirties, that the sun had just peeked out, and we were the first plane all day that would not need to be deiced.

Isn't that incredible? Wow! We serve an amazing God. Maybe someday I will write a book about the weather and share all of the verses I have discovered, along with many other weather-related stories. But for now, suffice it to say that God will reveal to us what even the weather is about, and as we yield to His direction, we will be blessed and have great experiences with Him in this realm. Allow me to share a couple of examples about Jesus in the Gospels, starting with John 11:1–44:

> Now a certain man was sick, Lazarus of Bethany, the town of Mary and her sister Martha. It was that Mary who anointed the Lord with fragrant oil and wiped His feet with her hair, whose brother Lazarus was sick. Therefore the sisters sent to Him, saying, "Lord, behold, he whom You love is sick."
>
> When Jesus heard that, He said, "This sickness is not unto death, but for the glory of God, that the Son of God may be glorified through it."
>
> Now Jesus loved Martha and her sister and Lazarus. So, when He heard that he was sick, He stayed two more days in the place where He was. Then after this He said to the disciples, "Let us go to Judea again."
>
> The disciples said to Him, "Rabbi, lately the Jews sought to stone You, and are You going there again?"
>
> Jesus answered, "Are there not twelve hours in the day? If anyone walks in the day, he does not stumble, because he sees the light of this world. But if one walks in the night, he stumbles, because the light is not in him." These things He said, and after that He said to them, "Our friend Lazarus sleeps, but I go that I may wake him up."

Then His disciples said, "Lord, if he sleeps he will get well." However, Jesus spoke of his death, but they thought that He was speaking about taking rest in sleep.

Then Jesus said to them plainly, "Lazarus is dead. And I am glad for your sakes that I was not there, that you may believe. Nevertheless let us go to him."

Then Thomas, who is called the Twin, said to his fellow disciples, "Let us also go, that we may die with Him."

So when Jesus came, He found that he had already been in the tomb four days. Now Bethany was near Jerusalem, about two miles away. And many of the Jews had joined the women around Martha and Mary, to comfort them concerning their brother.

Now Martha, as soon as she heard that Jesus was coming, went and met Him, but Mary was sitting in the house. Now Martha said to Jesus, "Lord, if You had been here, my brother would not have died. But even now I know that whatever You ask of God, God will give You."

Jesus said to her, "Your brother will rise again."

Martha said to Him, "I know that he will rise again in the resurrection at the last day."

Jesus said to her, "I am the resurrection and the life. He who believes in Me, though he may die, he shall live. And whoever lives and believes in Me shall never die. Do you believe this?"

She said to Him, "Yes, Lord, I believe that You are the Christ, the Son of God, who is to come into the world."

And when she had said these things, she went her way and secretly called Mary her sister, saying, "The Teacher has come and is calling for you." As soon as she heard that, she arose quickly and came to Him. Now Jesus had not yet come into the town, but was in the place where Martha met

Him. Then the Jews who were with her in the house, and comforting her, when they saw that Mary rose up quickly and went out, followed her, saying, "She is going to the tomb to weep there."

Then, when Mary came where Jesus was, and saw Him, she fell down at His feet, saying to Him, "Lord, if You had been here, my brother would not have died."

Therefore, when Jesus saw her weeping, and the Jews who came with her weeping, He groaned in the spirit and was troubled. And He said, "Where have you laid him?"

They said to Him, "Lord, come and see."

Jesus wept. Then the Jews said, "See how He loved him!"

And some of them said, "Could not this Man, who opened the eyes of the blind, also have kept this man from dying?"

Then Jesus, again groaning in Himself, came to the tomb. It was a cave, and a stone lay against it. Jesus said, "Take away the stone."

Martha, the sister of him who was dead, said to Him, "Lord, by this time there is a stench, for he has been dead four days."

Jesus said to her, "Did I not say to you that if you would believe you would see the glory of God?" Then they took away the stone from the place where the dead man was lying. And Jesus lifted up His eyes and said, "Father, I thank You that You have heard Me. And I know that You always hear Me, but because of the people who are standing by I said this, that they may believe that You sent Me." Now when He had said these things, He cried with a loud voice, "Lazarus, come forth!" And he who had died came out bound hand and foot with grave clothes, and his face was wrapped with a cloth. Jesus said to them, "Loose him, and let him go."

This is an amazing narrative, and I am sure you have probably heard some great messages about this story at some point in your lifetime. But I want you to think about something. John 5:19 says that Jesus only did what He saw His Father doing. And that is a pattern that we should follow too.

Here is what I believe: I believe that Jesus went from one prayer meeting to another, and performed ministry in-between.³ Since Jesus was a man of prayer, and we know He would often go away to be in prayer with His Father, and that He was indeed doing what He saw the Father doing, we then have to add this dimension to the story from John 11.

I believe that Jesus got the whole narrative in advance and that the Father added in some points that are not recorded for us. Obviously, I can't prove it, but I do believe it. I believe that the Father said something like this to Jesus: "Your friend Lazarus is going to get sick and then actually die, but don't worry about it because I have a plan. In fact, Your friends are going to accuse you of not caring, but I do have a plan. The Sadducees do not believe in a resurrection from the dead at all; whereas, the Pharisees do believe in one, but it has to happen within three days. So We are going to mess up their theology big time, and they are going to have a theophany in a brand new experience that will add more people to Our Kingdom." Verse forty-five says that many Jews were added to the kingdom that day as they believed. Isn't that wonderful?

I know what some of you are thinking: "Then, why did Jesus cry?" I honestly believe He might have been crying over their unbelief because He told them several times that Lazarus would wake up. No one seemed to remember this as they had their eyes set on the things that they could see in the natural rather than the things they could not see, in the realm of faith. I can't prove these things, but I believe them to be true because of the very nature of God. Why would Jesus cry over something that He knew was changing in just a few moments? He had previously prophesied that Lazarus would rise up. These are indeed strange prayers and strange answers, don't you agree?

Here is another one for you to consider that our pastor Jim Hart from Eagle's Nest Worship Center in Omaha, Nebraska, taught recently. The teaching is based on Mark 8:22–25:

> Then [Jesus] came to Bethsaida; and they brought a blind man to Him, and begged Him to touch him. So He took the blind man by the hand and led him out of the town. And when He had spit on his eyes and put

His hands on him, He asked him if he saw anything. And he looked up and said, "I see men like trees, walking." Then He put His hands on his eyes again and made him look up. And he was restored and saw everyone clearly.

Now, please pay attention to the following definitions Pastor Hart shared with me:

RESTORE: Greek Word *Apokathistemi*—to restore again. From Apo—cessation (final ceasing of action) and Kathistemi—to appoint or designate; to restore to a former condition by adding water.

CLEARLY: *Telagus*—far shining manner; Telagus is a combination of two words "telos" and "auge". Telos: a point aimed at – ultimate prophetic goal or result; Auge: Rays of light – radiance – break of the day.

In other words he saw things like this: He saw everyone in their ultimate final prophetic ending or goal, a result shining with radiance, a shining like the breaking of the day! It was as if the first view by seeing men like trees was like looking on a foggy day. But now with the anointed presence of Jesus, it was a new day and the vision was restored. But I really like the definition of the word *restore*: to restore to a former state by adding water. Seeing Jesus spit on a guy would be a strange thing to behold, but when you understand what was happening, then it all makes sense.

Jesus did what He saw the Father doing, and in this case the blind man then got to see what Jesus was doing too. As you read on, perhaps your vision will increase for what God is doing in your life today. I will tell you this for sure, there are no optical illusions with God.

Journey

Has God ever shared something with you that really sounded ridiculous? How did you respond? Did you give in to your own thoughts or give it up to God? What makes the difference in your life? Do you know how to discern what God is saying to you? If not, do you want to learn?

I will share more about this in later chapters as we continue the study times, but for now why don't you ask God to reveal a Scripture verse to you that would add value to your current situation in life right now? I believe that if you go to prayer and sincerely and genuinely ask Him for a verse or two, He will inspire you to look up certain verses in your Bible that will demonstrate to you or share with you something important that will be useful to you as you work through this aspect in your life. It doesn't even have to be a current issue in your life that He is addressing. Rather, something could be coming up in your life that He knows if you follow His advice and leading it will turn out even better for you.

I have experienced many of these examples, and I am confident that what God did for me He will also do for you. Trust is a Must! Will you trust Him now as you stop and pray? Ask God to show you what He is doing in the situation you are praying about, and then trust Him when you hear back. Often God is working behind the scenes on our behalf, and even though we can't see Him, He is working, fixing, completing, healing, providing, and yes, even restoring. So if you don't mind a little spit, you may just see things differently from this point on.

CHAPTER FOUR

STUDY TIME: PART 2

I concluded the first study time in Chapter Two with the following thoughts and instructions:

> Matthew 15:11 says that it is not what goes into the mouth that defiles a man, but what comes out. And Matthew 11:34 proclaims that out of the abundance of the heart, the mouth speaks.
>
> A person's life will always go in the direction of his or her most dominant thought. Proverbs 23:7 says, "As a man thinks in his heart so is he," and Judges 8:21 says, "As a man is, so is his strength." Let's combine those, and we see that what we are thinking about determines our strength.
>
> In 2 Corinthians 10:1–6 we read the following:
>
> Now I, Paul, myself am pleading with you by the meekness and gentleness of Christ—who in presence am lowly among you, but being absent am bold toward you. But I beg you that when I am present I may not be bold with that confidence by which I intend to be bold against some, who think of us as if we walked according to the flesh. For though we walk in the flesh, we do not war according to the flesh. For the weapons of our warfare are not carnal but mighty in God for pulling down strongholds, casting down arguments and every high thing that exalts itself against the knowledge of God, bringing every thought into captivity to the obedience of Christ, and being ready to punish all disobedience when your obedience is fulfilled.
>
> Please notice the phrase "bringing every thought into captivity, to the

obedience of Christ." This is a critical statement. Thoughts, if not dealt with, can lead to destruction. Let me illustrate. Do you remember why water came out of the bottle? Because there was water in the bottle. Why do violence and foul language come out of a person? Because violence and foul language are in a person. And where does it all begin? With a thought.

Watch and follow this progression:

A thought becomes a consideration, which then becomes a decision. Let's stop right here and break it down further. Perhaps you have just started a diet and you are tempted by a left over sweet roll in the fridge. You think about it, consider it, and make a decision. Yes, you will eat it or no, you will skip it. But the process begins with a thought.

There is a story of such an incident in which a man who had started a diet just a few days earlier was driving to work and saw in the display case of his favorite bakery a delicious chocolate éclair oozing with Boston cream along with luscious whipped cream and a cherry on top. Boy, did it look good! So the man prayed a quick prayer and said, "Lord, even though I have just started this diet, I sure would like to eat that éclair. If it would be within Your will that I eat that wonderful confectionary, please let a parking space open up in front of the bakery." Sure enough, on the seventh time around the block, one opened up. Wow, what an incredible answer to prayer. So, who is hungry now?

Here is a quote by Blaise Pascal to consider: "Man's greatness lies in his power of thought." I would add that those great thoughts must be centered on the kingdom of God. Otherwise, they produce a proud look, which I will address in just a bit.

So we have a thought becoming a consideration leading to a decision. This then leads to an act, followed by an act repeated, which then becomes a habit; and that, my chocolate éclair-loving friends, turns into a stronghold. You might inquire, what is a stronghold? A stronghold is anything that has a strong hold on you. So I say let Jesus and the power of the Holy Spirit have a strong hold on you.

Years ago, when I was a pastor in Kansas, I was at our county fair and a guy had an accident on a corner near the fair. I happened to walk by this fender bender and knew the man. He approached me and asked me to go get his brother in the fairgrounds, and then he asked, "Can you get me a beer too?" In fact, he asked me several times to get him a beer but only included his brother once more. All the while, he was kind of tipsy while walking and probably was under the power of other previous beers that afternoon. His thoughts were controlled by the alcohol more than the fact that he had just been in a car accident.

Zig Ziglar, in his book *Born to Win*, quotes Frank Outlaw with this progressive sequential thought: "Watch your thoughts; they become your words. Watch your words; they become actions. Watch your actions; they become habits. Watch your habits; they become your character. Watch your character; for it becomes your destiny."[4]

Romans 8:6 instructs us to be spiritually minded, which produces life, and to avoid being carnally-minded, which ends in death. I shared this in more detail in my book *Downloads from Heaven*. The word *carne* is a Latin word meaning meat. Hence, *chili con carne* is chili with meat. In a sense, God is saying, "Don't be a meathead." Keep your thoughts centered on the kingdom of God, and not so much on things that pertain to this world. Look more at Jesus and less at your own circumstances. In his book *Healing Broken Lives and Relationships,* Donald Phillips wrote that we should "gaze … at God and glance at the problem."[5]

The words of a great Christian hymn, penned by Helen Lemmel in 1922, give all of us a clearer view of these helpful suggestions. Look at the refrain of "Turn Your Eyes Upon Jesus":

Turn your eyes upon Jesus,
Look full in His wonderful face,
And the things of earth will grow strangely dim,
In the light of His glory and grace.

Go ahead and sing it, I know you want to. It'll be great. If there are others in the room, just sing it softly. No one will give it a second thought. (Oops, there's that word *thought*!) Maybe not!

Let's shift gears here and read through 2 Samuel 6 starting with verse 12 to the end of the chapter.

Now it was told King David, saying, "The LORD has blessed the house of Obed-Edom and all that belongs to him, because of the ark of God." So David went and brought up the ark of God from the house of Obed-Edom to the City of David with gladness. And so it was, when those bearing the ark of the Lord had gone six paces, that he sacrificed oxen and fatted sheep. Then David danced before the Lord with all his might; and David was wearing a linen ephod. So David and all the house of Israel brought up the ark of the Lord with shouting and with the sound of the trumpet.

Now as the ark of the Lord came into the City of David, Michal, Saul's daughter, looked through a window and saw King David leaping and whirling before the Lord; and she despised him in her heart. So they brought the ark of the Lord, and set it in its place in the midst of the tabernacle that David had erected for it. Then David offered burnt offerings and peace offerings before the Lord. And when David had finished offering burnt offerings and peace offerings, he blessed the people in the name of the Lord of hosts. Then he distributed among all the people, among the whole multitude of Israel, both the women and the men, to everyone a loaf of bread, a piece of meat, and a cake of raisins. So all the people departed, everyone to his house.

Then David returned to bless his household. And Michal the daughter of Saul came out to meet David, and said, "How glorious was the king of Israel today, uncovering himself today in the eyes of the maids of his servants, as one of the base fellows shamelessly uncovers himself!"

So David said to Michal, "It was before the Lord, who chose me instead of your father and all his house, to appoint me ruler over the people of the Lord, over Israel. Therefore I will play music before the Lord. And I will be even more undignified than this, and will be humble in my own sight. But as for the maidservants of whom you have spoken, by them I will be held in honor."

Therefore Michal the daughter of Saul had no children to the day of her death.

This is a great story with tremendous examples that relate so well to this study time, and I know you are going to receive a lot of revelation from it. In fact, I am going to pray for you right now.

Dear Lord,

I believe that the people reading this chapter right now could use some special revelation for their lives. Would You please release that revelation to them as they continue with the reading of this chapter? I invite Your Holy Spirit to bring comfort, aid, and peace to their lives, but also to challenge them to greater goals, aspirations and kingdom enhancements as they read the rest of this chapter and even the rest of the book.

May this story in 2 Samuel reveal truth and inspire change that will enable each person reading this to really go after You in a special and unique way. I pray that the words that I share and the anointing that is on each page will transform thinking, rearrange schedules, and set in motion practical opportunities for mindsets to be changed and life as they know it to be forever set on a new journey and pattern that releases power in their lives.

Lord, I believe You can and want to do this very thing, as I was prompted to write this prayer, not in my notes, but just as I was writing this section of the book. I thank You, Jesus, for all that You are to us and all that You will become for us. I am grateful and look forward to what is next. Amen!

Okay, now ask, "What's Next?" Go ahead and ask it. You can do it. This is easier than singing a few moments ago. Did you ask it? I believe you did.

Okay, I am glad you asked.

King David was bringing the Ark of the Lord back into his kingdom because wherever the Ark was, the presence of the Lord was there too, and in that realm was great favor. King David was excited about this, so he began to dance before the Lord. He wasn't wearing his kingly garments, and in modern day vernacular, was probably down to his P.E. shorts and a tank top. His wife, who was called Saul's daughter in three separate places, including verses 16, 20, and 23, was ridiculing, scolding, mocking, and definitely criticizing him. Where should she have been, and what was motivating her to do this? Well, she should have been down on the corner (out on the street) where the King was singing, making music with his feet. (Forgive me,

Creedence Clearwater Revival, but I am pressing for a different and lasting revival with Jesus.)

It's interesting that on three occasions she was called the daughter of Saul, the daughter of Saul, the daughter of Saul. I have previously learned that when children get married, the biblical principle is that they are to leave their parents and cleave to their new mate. But Michal seemed to be cleaving to her late father, King Saul. The problem was in her mind, specifically in her thoughts.

She continued to think like her dad and act like her dad, which she undoubtedly observed on many occasions growing up, seeing King Saul go after God for awhile, but then back up a few steps and retreat from the Lord too. These patterns had been engrained in her from early on, and were certainly tough patterns to break.

David, while being a king, and dancing on the street, recognized that there was a greater King, so he submitted to Him to display honor. Michal declared that his actions were dishonorable, but David addressed this in verse 22 and stressed that the honor of dancing before the Lord God was something not to be taken lightly.

Michal was throwing one accusation after another at David, but David responded with meekness, yet with strong leadership qualities, trying to convince her that what he was doing had been thought out and planned as an act of worship. He emphasized that it was the Lord who chose him and anointed him, so he was simply responding back with praise, thanksgiving, and glory to the true King.

Also in verse 22, David let Michal know that he intended to be even more undignified than that. The word *undignified* comes from the word *dignified*, and the word *dignified* comes from the word *dignity*. The first definition in the dictionary for dignity is pride. I believe David was saying that he was getting rid of all the pride, including every prideful thought, and was going all out after God, regardless of how he may dress or act, or what others may think. In James 4:6, we learn that God resists the proud and gives grace to the humble, and in Proverbs 6:16–17 God shares that even a proud look is an abomination. I am personally grateful for the friends who approached me lovingly along the way and showed me where I was walking in too much pride. We all need some friends like that.

As David addressed Michal, it's as if he was saying, "You ain't seen nothing yet, baby. If you think this is bad or tough, just hang on, because more is coming."

Then a very sad and distressing bit of information was shared. Michal had no children until the day of her death. This is depressing, for sure. Most married women want children, and it is a God-given command to be fruitful and replenish the earth. Plus, if a son is born, he may be the next leader, and that brings great honor to the mother too. But Michal would see no children in her family lines.

There are two possible reasons for Michal's barrenness that I came up with. First, it's possible God just allowed her to be barren for her entire life for not sharing in David's street dance that special day as the Ark of the Lord was brought back into the kingdom. But maybe there is another explanation.

Maybe David simply said to his wife, if you are going to carry on this trait of being so much like your father, then I will not sleep with you or be intimate with you. My intimacy is first with my Lord and if you can't share that with me, then I won't share any personal intimacy with you either; thus, she had no children to the day of her death.

Maybe you have known people who point fingers at those who are pressing in for more of God, who perhaps look at certain manifestations or spiritual gifts with accusing thoughts and words, and who just don't carry any new life from Jesus. Perhaps you know folks who at one time were hot for God, or were on the cutting edge of revelation and teaching, or perhaps were making great strides and accomplishments in a local church as it pertained to the kingdom of God, but now you hardly ever see them, and when asked to pray or lead a study group, they always defer. There is no new spiritual life left in them, which has prevented their spiritual walk from growing stronger and stronger with Jesus.

What happened? It probably was motivated by a thought. They became judgmental and critical, and slowly but surely lost friends, kingdom authority, and kingdom power, only now to be relegated to an occasional memory of the past, yet complaining, pointing fingers, and blaming someone else for their situation.

Abraham Lincoln said, "All my life I have tried to pluck a thistle and plant a flower wherever the flower would grow in thought and mind." Link that together with the mindset of Alex Haley, author of *Roots*, in which he wrote and lived by the principle of these six words: "Find the good and praise it."[6]

The Apostle Paul said it this way in Philippians 4:8: "Finally, brethren, whatever things are true, whatever things are noble, whatever things are just, whatever things are pure, whatever things are lovely, whatever things are of good report, if there is any virtue and if there is anything praiseworthy—meditate on these things." The same verse from The New Living Translation states: "And now, dear brothers and sisters, one final thing. Fix your thoughts on what is true, and honorable, and right, and pure, and lovely, and admirable. Think about things that are excellent and worthy of praise."

God knew that our thoughts could either promote the kingdom or divide it, so He gave the warning in 2 Corinthians 10 to take every thought captive to the obedience of Christ so that no unholy or cowardly thought would have dominion over you or me. He instructed us on how to proceed in life with godly thoughts and ideas that regenerate the kingdom of God and promote Christian unity where He loves to command a blessing! If only Michal, Saul's daughter and David's wife, had done the same thing. Her theology would have changed her theophany experience.

Proverbs 15:33 in the Message says, "Fear-of-God is a school in skilled living—first you learn humility, then you experience glory." King David declared that he was getting rid of the pride. Michal continued in prideful remarks. If you want to experience true glory in the presence of the Lord, you must take the prideful thoughts captive and walk in humility that will lead to a walk that is filled with daily new life blessings.

Journey

It would be difficult to reduce this chapter down to a specific task for your journey, as there was so much meat contained in it, so let's simply do this: Take a few moments right now to jot down perhaps three areas of your life in which you are acting prideful and need God's correction and new direction. Or, list three negative thought patterns that continue to plague you in your walk with God and that seem to create barriers hindering God from working in your life.

As I suggested, write them down and then begin to pray and ask God to help you move past these patterns so that a new sequence of steps begins to be developed to the point that you are soon able to see your steps of faith as if you are walking in the mirror image of Jesus (see Romans 8:29).

Chapter 8 of Tom Newberry's book *The 4:8 Principle* is titled "Junk-Proof Your Mind." By taking the steps above, you will initiate God's strategies to accomplish that very thing. What junk needs to be removed from your thought life? What mental images have plagued you and ruled your mind far too long? Make time right now to take small steps toward the removal of these items and begin to transform your mind and convert it to what God intended for you. More information will be discussed on this topic in chapter seven.

CHAPTER FIVE

BEING UNCOMMON

HOW would you like to see your offering multiplied 1000 times? You are going to love the "Dime Story," so keep reading! Do you think you could kneel at the curb with a total stranger at an airport and pray with him to have a born again experience with Jesus? Read on, my friend.

Booker T. Washington said, "Excellence is to do a common thing in an uncommon way."

My banana story in a previous chapter is a great example of being uncommon. Couple that with the Target story, and you begin to see that God does things differently for folks and is not into cookie-cutter ministry. Jesus actually prayed for six different blind guys six different ways. Yet, we have our methods and our ways. The American church seems to love to copy others rather than spend the time pressing in to God to discover how He might have us do ministry. We love the forty ways to this and the thirty ways to that, as well as the twelve steps that will set you free in this area and the seventeen weeks of evangelism methods, only to discover that while God used those in other locations and the anointing was on them for those situations, it may or may not be there for your situation, because He is doing it differently with you.

I have frequently told church leaders that just because another local church has a thriving young adult ministry does not necessarily mean you are to have one too. Or just because a church near you has a Christian day school or preschool does not mean your church should have one too. We are to be unique and uncommon with a common faith and different expressions, following the presence of God in our area, location, and neighborhood.

I already shared all of the details about the first car we gave away, but the second car was totally different in that we gave it to good friends. We reduced the price significantly from what we had paid for it just two weeks earlier and gave them an interest-free loan for a short time so that they could acquire this car. God was in both situations, but the procedure and process was totally different.

First Peter 2:9 launches this chapter with these words: "But you are a chosen generation, a royal priesthood, a holy nation, His own special people, that you may proclaim the praises of Him who called you out of darkness into His marvelous light." Years ago, when I was on staff at a church in Houston as a youth pastor, I gave the Easter sunrise message and used this text. I remember I titled the sermon "Weird and Unique." I still like that title, but I have tamed it down some for this chapter, referring to it instead as being uncommon. This uncommonness reminds me of another message I taught called "Moving from Normal Church to Normal Christianity."

I think that many would agree that most of the Church in America has lost influence and is barely tolerated rather than being appreciated. This is an exaggeration, but we have churches on every corner, yet not enough authority to see much really happen or be changed. Jesus said in Luke 9:1–2 that He was extending to us power and authority. Would you say that out loud? "Power and Authority."

Power is the ability, might, and strength to complete a task, but authority is the right to use that power. I am sure you have seen a movie or perhaps a real-life news drama in which a police unit or S.W.A.T. team is working to end a violent standoff. In the scene there is often a well-trained police officer who is an excellent marksman with a rifle. This officer generally has an earpiece and a mouthpiece and is in communication with his commander. Often you will hear conversation that might go like this: The marksman says, "I can take him now," but through the earpiece comes the command, "No, don't shoot. We want to take the criminal alive." The marksman replies, "But he is within my sight and I can shoot him now," but the command once again comes back, telling him to hold his fire.

The marksman officer has an extreme amount of power in his hand, enough to actually take a life, but he does not have the authority to bend his index finger in the middle. He does not have the authority for the slightest bend of his finger. Isn't that interesting?

God has given us power and authority, but few want to take it and use it for the kingdom. I like what Pastor Bill Johnson from Bethel Church in

Redding, California, says about this subject. He says that power is the ability to ride a wave, but authority is the ability to create a wave.

Since I travel so much, I get to see a lot of *church*, and it's not all that pretty. There are indeed some great churches out there who are pressing in for more of the kingdom, and for that I am very grateful. They are flowing in the anointing of God with power and authority and making a difference in their spheres of influence, and that is a big "praise the Lord," for sure. But I hear reports from friends who tell me that their church is boring, uneventful, and routine. My son Jason and I once attended a revival, and we commented on how it had become predictable. I do not want to ever become predictable. The church should be one of the most uncommon places on the planet, but due to an unwillingness to yield to the things of God, the church has frequently become so much like the world that you often can't tell the difference. So much of the church looks alike, acts alike, sounds alike, and smells alike. In fact, much of it stinks because it has moved from the freedom and life of Jesus to religious bondage.

From the viewpoint of an un-churched or de-churched person, what is the difference between the church you attend and another one down the street, besides simple location? Again, to the un-churched and untrained spiritual eyes, what is the difference between a Methodist, Lutheran, Presbyterian, Baptist, Pentecostal, Nazarene, Friends, Quaker, Full Gospel, Catholic, Episcopal, Evangelical Free, Assembly of God, Foursquare, Word of Faith, or any other named church you can think of?

The church is supposed to be filled with people who are in love with Jesus, sharing Jesus, and proclaiming Jesus. I believe many are, but many aren't, too. Mark 1:11 says, "Then a voice came from heaven saying, 'You are My beloved Son in whom I am well pleased.'" But when God looks collectively at all of the churches, do you think He says the same thing? I am not convinced He does. There is nothing about most churches that is unique, peculiar, weird, or uncommon that would set them apart from other churches. There is no real distinction.

Look at Wendy's, McDonald's, Burger King, What-a-Burger, In and Out, and Jack in the Box. Compare Wal-Mart, K-Mart, Target, and Sears. How about Sam's and Costco? Perhaps look at Shell, Exxon, Chevron, Sinclair, and Conoco. The list goes on and on, depending on the category that you come up with. Yet most people could tell you right away what the difference is between McDonald's and Wendy's or Wal-Mart and Target. Why is that? Because in their commonness, they also have unique features that make them uncommon compared to each other.

But for the most part, the church is just as sick, just as in debt, and has just as many problems, broken relationships, burdens, and cares as anyone in the world who is not in the church. There is just as much over-the-counter dependence in the church as in the world, as well as just as much drunkenness. And the divorce rate is higher in the church.

So, translate this: I have often stated, that Christians invite people to their church, but the un-churched person looks at them and says, "You want me to give up my Sunday morning sleeping in, brunch time, or golf tee, and come to your church to be just like you, act just like you, and give you my money, but there is no return for my buck?" They see lives not changed, so why would the unchurched want give up their time to do that? What is the point?

Think about it. You don't shop at Target because it reminds you of Sears. You don't eat at Outback Steakhouse because it reminds you of Ruby Tuesday, and you don't stay at Holiday Inn because it reminds you of Marriott. It's the difference that makes the difference. And to the un-churched, we all look alike: boring, dull, no power, and definitely no authority.

Are you aware that, according to the Barna Research Group, there are 80 million Americans who have no church at all and then another 40 million Americans who have a church home, but don't attend?[7] That is a staggering statistic. One of the main reasons for this is because we aren't uncommon, and the reason we aren't uncommon is because we have lost the ability to yield to our Father, our God, and our King. One of the reasons we have lost that is because, as Americans, we want our say and our vote. We want our opinions to be heard, so we have Burger King theology, in that we want it our way and we want it fast.

I want to flow in the river of God, go where the river goes, and flow where the river flows, just as the words flow in the song "Deep Cries Out" by William Mathews.[8]

I've got a river of living water
A fountain that never will run dry
It's open Heavens You're releasing
And we will never be denied

Cause we're stirring up deep, deep wells
We're stirring up deep, deep waters
We're going to dance in the river, dance in the river
Cause we're stirring up deep, deep wells
We're stirring up deep, deep waters
We're going to jump in the river, jump in the river
And everybody singing now

Deep cries out to, deep cries out to
Deep cries out to, deep cries out to
So we cry out to, we cry out to, You Jesus

We're falling into deeper waters, calling out to You
We're walking into deeper waters, going after You

If He goes to the left, then we'll go to the left
And if He goes to the right, then we'll go to the right
We're going to jump, jump, jump, jump in the river
Jump, jump, jump, jump, everybody
If He goes to the left, then we'll go to the left
And if He goes to the right, then we'll go to the right
We're going to dance, dance, dance, dance in the river
Dance, dance, dance, dance, everybody
If He goes to the left then we'll go to the left
And if He goes to the right then we'll go to the right
We're going to shout, shout, shout, shout in the river
Shout, shout, shout, shout in the river, everybody.

Again, I am reiterating that Jesus only did what He saw the Father doing, as given in John 5:19. You and I both know that each day for Jesus, as recorded in the four Gospels, was anything but routine. His earthly biography contained a swirl of activity, with preaching and teaching, combined with evangelism, confronting religious structures, healing the sick, raising the dead, proclaiming the kingdom, training disciples, and being with common people—even when it was uncommon to do so.

There is a story of a race between a rabbit, a squirrel, and a duck. The race would include three categories: running, climbing, and swimming. After all three events, the rabbit was celebrated as a significant runner, the squirrel was celebrated as a significant climber, and the duck was celebrated as a significant swimmer. However, they were not celebrated in what the other had accomplished. The rabbit could not climb and the squirrel could not swim and the duck could not run. (Note: This was obviously before the Aflac Duck commercials.)

All three were celebrated and honored for their significance. This allowed for the differences to define them and not confine them. All three were successful in uncommon giftings and abilities, unique to their own environment and personal status. I believe that when we stay focused on the mission of Jesus, walking within the realm of our measure of rule and spheres of influence, we will be appreciated and celebrated, but if we stay common, just like the rest, we will merely be tolerated and ultimately eliminated.

Every life has an uncommon message. When presenting this message or one similar to it by theme and design, I will have the people in the congregation, school, or business, turn to each other and repeat after me saying, "When God made you, He said, 'I will never do that again.'" I actually did this as a toast in a family wedding once too. This always gets a good laugh, but the reality is that we have our own fingerprints, DNA, and physiological footprint that is distinctly different from every other person on the planet, and this is by design by our Creator. Yet, when we band together, we often try to make everything the same.

Several years ago, I hosted discipleship groups in my home once a month on Saturday mornings. I had ten men come for ninety minutes with a thirty-minute break following, and then ten women came, along with my wife, for ninety more minutes. We had a great time learning and applying biblical truths to our lives. At one point a lady from Council Bluffs, Iowa, which is just across the Missouri River from Omaha, contacted me, asking if she could join the women's group. I inquired as to why she wanted to join, and she told me that she wanted to increase her prayer life and the value of prayer with her family. When she contacted me, she could not even pray with family members at home, but desired to grow in that area and become more courageous.

A few months after joining our group, she found herself studying for our class at a local McDonald's, and a young man approached her and asked what she was doing. This young African American was an employee of that particular McDonald's. She told him what she was studying, and after a short conversation, she offered to pray with this young man and then went back a week later to follow up with him.

In a very short amount of time, she went from not being able to pray with her family to now praying with a stranger in a public place. She was a middle-aged lady praying with a young man who was 18, and she was White and he was Black. Wow, look at how far she had grown, and then she went back to follow up with him too. Now this was an uncommon action because many churches will center in on attendance, but few major on discipleship. Jesus commanded us to make disciples. A true disciple has been made not just by pouring your life into someone else. That would be called mentoring, which is also a tremendous, gracious, and learning act. But a disciple is only formed when, after pouring your life into someone else, that person then goes and begins to pour his or her life into the life of still another person. This is what that lady from Council Bluffs did.

It's time for us to move back into that weird and unique position of being uncommon so that we can manifest, display, and share the kingdom of God with common tenets of faith but different expressions that will encourage others to be hungry for God, maybe without even knowing why. It's time to make disciples and see the kingdom of God grow systematically but also at a more rapid pace than what many church growth advocates suggest. To be honest, I am not very interested in church growth, but I am highly interested in kingdom growth. I recently told a pastor from a church in another state during a Skype call that I am seeker-sensitive to get people in the doors, but after they are there, I am Holy Spirit sensitive to equip, enable, anoint, and then release those same people into what I will call on-fire-for-Jesus believers who have a strategy and a plan to see others experience the same thing, with similar kingdom results.

So let's look at some uncommon stories from the Bible with uncommon messages that we can learn and glean from to set us on a course that will require us to yield all the more and to be willing and obedient all the more, yet with a new understanding and appreciation for how God may be working in and through us to adopt more sons and daughters into His family. Are you up for the challenge? If you are, then get in the river of God, start swimming, and say, "Aflac!"

Luke 5:1–6 is a great place to start with uncommon directions:

> So it was, as the multitude pressed about Him to hear the word of God, that He stood by the Lake of Gennesaret, and saw two boats standing by the lake; but the fishermen had gone from them and were washing their nets. Then He got into one of the boats, which was Simon's, and asked him to put out a little from the land. And He sat down and taught the multitudes from the boat.
>
> When He had stopped speaking, He said to Simon, "Launch out into the deep and let down your nets for a catch."
>
> But Simon answered and said to Him, "Master, we have toiled all night and caught nothing; nevertheless at Your word I will let down the net." And when they had done this, they caught a great number of fish, and their net was breaking.

These are uncommon directions.

Can you imagine making this request? If nothing else, the guys were tired, having fished all night in the dark, and now were cleaning their nets. Casting them again would mean more cleaning, more work, and less sleep until the next night. Yet, they responded to the word of God. Mary did the same thing in Luke 1 (I will share more on that later, but she also responded to the word of God, and not the impossibility of the situation).

Several years ago, I was at a local church for a Sunday evening service, and God gave me a prophetic word for the congregation that I felt I was to share with the senior pastor. I started to go forward to share this word, but the Lord spoke to me and told me not to go forward, but to wait for the pastor to turn around, point at me, and ask me if I had a word for him. So I was waiting through the service, and there was a lot of worship going on. Finally, the pastor, who was not on the platform but in the front row, turned around and I thought, "This is it." But he only got a glass of water and went back to worship.

Later in the service he turned around again, but it was to whisper something to one of his other leaders. Then he decided to lie down on the floor and worship. At this point I was thinking, *I have heard wrong*, and I felt like I should go up and share with him. But God clearly told me once again to wait, so I waited and waited and waited. Finally, he got up and turned around, and I thought, *Okay, I am glad I waited*, only to see him get his Bible and begin to read it. Worship was still going on.

He then got up and raised his hands for a few moments and then suddenly turned around, pointed directly at me, and asked, "Do you have a word for me?" I immediately nodded my head and went up and shared it with him, and he acted on it immediately, stopping worship and implementing what I had shared with him.

These were undoubtedly uncommon directions because I knew the pastor well and could have easily approached him at any time during the service, but God had another plan.

Let's now examine John 5:1–9:

> After this there was a feast of the Jews, and Jesus went up to Jerusalem. Now there is in Jerusalem by the Sheep Gate a pool, which is called in Hebrew, Bethesda, having five porches. In these lay a great multitude of sick people, blind, lame, paralyzed, waiting for the moving of the water. For an angel went down at a certain time into the pool and stirred up the water; then whoever stepped in first, after the stirring of the water, was made well of whatever disease he had. Now a certain man was there who had an infirmity thirty-eight years. When Jesus saw him lying there, and knew that he already had been in that condition a long time, He said to him, "Do you want to be made well?"
>
> The sick man answered Him, "Sir, I have no man to put me into the pool when the water is stirred up; but while I am coming, another steps down before me."
>
> Jesus said to him, "Rise, take up your bed and walk." And immediately the man was made well, took up his bed, and walked.
>
> And that day was the Sabbath.

I love this story and have taught from it many times. The question that Jesus asks is an uncommon question: Do you want to be made well? What a funny question to ask to a guy who is in a group of folks in an environment where people are all waiting to get well.

One time when I was walking out of the dentist's office after a rather expensive procedure, I was kind of complaining in my mind about the cost and then contemplating other expenses at home, including things that needed to be repaired and the recent license fees on my car. I was just rehearsing over and over all of the financial problems I was facing, and in the middle of all that, God interrupted my thoughts and asked me this question: "Are you blessed?" I literally stopped in my tracks and responded, "Yes." And then God asked, "So what's the problem?" End of conversation. From that moment, that uncommon question changed my perspective for the rest of the day, the week, and the month. You might ask if the bills disappeared, and they did not; but my viewpoint of God's presence in my life had changed, and I was and am sincerely blessed.

There's a bit more in this story that I would like to uncover while we are here. Jesus asked the man if he wanted to get well, and his response was one of discouragement. He simply stated that he had no one to help him in the water, but when he tried, others beat him to it. He answered a question that Jesus did not ask. And he gave excuses too. Think about it: Those who were at this pool all needed a helper to get in the pool because of their condition. So you can imagine that if their helper went into town to the local McDonald's that the person who needed healing probably said something like this: "Stay within shouting distance so you can run back if the water is stirred up." Or if their helper had gone to the port-a-potty, a similar conversation probably took place. Because each person who was there, being blind, lame, or paralyzed, most likely needed a helper.

So what were these sick people doing when the water was calm? Most likely, they were looking at their helper and looking at the water, then looking at their helper, then at the water. This scenario kept happening over and over because they wanted to get well.

The American Church is like this too. We look at the water, which can be translated as a method; and we look at the helper, which can be translated as the anointed man of God. The church loves methods and the people love to have someone with an anointing break through for them. Interestingly enough, Jesus came on the scene and no one else seemed to notice that this man got well outside of the method of the water being stirred up. Surely, those who were near this man knew him. He had been there a long time, and surely those you were sitting near would be people you would get to know. But there is no evidence that any of those near him even remotely saw that he got up and was now walking and most likely shouting. Why? Because they were too busy looking at the water and looking at their helper. And here Jesus Himself came on the scene, and they missed Him. Wow, what a mistake. We can easily identify and wonder how such a blunder could happen. Yet I believe it happens in churches across the country all the time because congregations have their menu and their program. Even though some leaders will stop and pray at the beginning, "Lord, have Your way," when He shows up, they miss Him because they are looking the wrong direction.

God knew I was mentally looking the wrong direction when I was complaining about my bills, so He brought a course correction with His question, "Are you blessed?" It was an uncommon question but one that definitely straightened me out. Is He asking you an uncommon question right now? Has He asked you one in the past? Don't wait too long to answer Him. He has answers for you and me, often working behind the scenes on our behalf so that our life will flow with the abundant life that Jesus talked about in John 10, if we will only respond to what He is offering us.

From Mark 12:41–44 we read the next uncommon story. It goes like this:

> Now Jesus sat opposite the treasury and saw how the people put money into the treasury. And many who were rich put in much. Then one poor widow came and threw in two mites, which make a quadrans. So He called His disciples to Himself and said to them, "Assuredly, I say to you that this poor widow has put in more than all those who have given to the treasury; for they all put in out of their abundance, but she out of her poverty put in all that she had, her whole livelihood."

This is an uncommon contribution. It's not a big contribution, but it is recorded in Scripture, so there must be something significant from the story for us to learn.

Back in 1999 when I was the pastor of a church in Texas, God spoke to us and told us to move to Omaha. Through a series of events, we acted on that word, including resigning from the church I was the pastor of and waiting for instructions on how to get to Omaha.

On the very weekend that I was finally finished at that local church, another pastor in the area called me up on a Sunday morning, inviting me to his church. He offered to have me work at his church in a variety of ways and places, further stating that he would take monthly love offerings for me as a way to bless me. He went on to say that regardless of how long it took my house to sell, whether two weeks or two months or two years, he would be happy to have the help and willing to facilitate these love offerings for me as well.

So in September I agreed to this plan, and off we went to help. True to his word, each month he took an offering for me and my family, except during December, he apparently forgot. I never said anything and just kept on working. Keep in mind that December is obviously Christmas with more expenses, plus my birthday and our son's birthday, and we still had our house payment and utility bills, etc. Also, my wife had resigned the previous year from her teaching position at a local Christian school, as we felt we were to home school our son that year, not knowing that God would be instructing us to move to Omaha.

At this point, it was January, and still no love offering. On the way out the door to church on the third Sunday of January, I saw a dime on the kitchen counter, and I did something I hardly ever do, which is carry change in my pocket. But on that day, I picked up the dime and put it in my pants pocket.

At church, they did what every church does in some way or another, and that is that they took up the offering. I really had little to give and no tithe as we had not received a love offering now in seven weeks, but God reminded me of the dime in my pocket, and He challenged me to place the dime in the offering plate, saying that He would multiply it by 1000. I did some quick math and calculated that would be one hundred dollars. I then had a thought about the ten dollars in my wallet, and if that was multiplied 1000 times how much that would be. But this was followed by a further consideration that obedience is better than sacrifice. So even though I felt somewhat conspicuous, I dropped the dime in the offering plate that morning.

A few days later, someone came over and gave me $200. Now, that was more than 1000 times the dime, so this was a great blessing. The next week in the same church, they were taking up an offering for some friends of ours who were going to the mission field in India, and I looked at my wife, and said, "We got double what I thought we were going to get last week, so let's give the $100 for this couple to go to India, and live on the $100. Keep in mind that it had now been eight weeks and our income for eight weeks was only $200.

But we freely gave the $100 gift to missions, and later that week I was invited to visit someone and share and pray with them, and when I was about to leave, they decided to give me a $1000 check. Wow, isn't God good? For us, these were two demonstrations of more uncommon contributions, just like the story above in Mark 12.

Are you up for one more? Let's study Mark 6:32–38:

So they departed to a deserted place in the boat by themselves.

But the multitudes saw them departing, and many knew Him and ran there on foot from all the cities. They arrived before them and came together to Him. And Jesus, when He came out, saw a great multitude and was moved with compassion for them, because they were like sheep not having a shepherd. So He began to teach them many things. When the day was now far spent, His disciples came to Him and said, "This is a deserted place, and already the hour is late. Send them away, that they may go into the surrounding country and villages and buy themselves bread; for they have nothing to eat."

But He answered and said to them, "You give them something to eat."

And they said to Him, "Shall we go and buy two hundred denarii worth of bread and give them something to eat?"

But He said to them, "How many loaves do you have? Go and see."

And when they found out they said, "Five, and two fish."

This is definitely an uncommon request. I have a lot more to teach on this subject in one of my CD teachings titled "Lessons from the Beach," but let me just say that the discipleship training was definitely a process for these men, and most likely it is for me and you too.

Years ago, I was attending an evangelism conference in Tulsa, Oklahoma, and when you have attended such an event, you want to try out what you have learned. So as my hotel van driver was taking me back to the airport, I was witnessing to this young man. As we neared the airport, I knew that my time was limited, so I asked him if he would like to invite Jesus to be a part of his life. He responded that he definitely would, but that we needed an altar. I responded, stating we did not have an altar, but maybe we could use the dashboard of the van. He said he had a better idea.

So I waited, and as we came to a stop at the airport, he got out to open the back of the van and unload my suitcase. As I got out of the van, he then turned the suitcase on its side on the curb and stated that this could be our altar. He then invited me to kneel at this airport altar made of a suitcase on the curb with hundreds of people walking by. Wow, this was an unusual request, but I thought, *Hey, why not?* So we knelt and prayed, and I took his name and phone number and later shared it with a pastor friend in Tulsa to follow up with him.

What would have happened if I had not yielded in each of these cases? What would the results have been? I believe that many things might have turned out differently, and most likely would not be included here in this book as a testimony for you to read. But my previous journey is now contributing to your present journey, and hopefully that trend continues as you also will contribute to someone else's spiritual journey with Jesus.

Journey

In the very last part of Revelation 19:10, we read, "The testimony of Jesus is the spirit of prophecy." This uncommon chapter, along with the previous ones, is filled with personal testimonies, some from me and some from others. And Jesus lives in me, so the testimonies are His and demonstrate how He is working in my life. But as you read and listen to a testimony, you should take it beyond just hearing a good report. That is okay, but there is more, in that each testimony releases a prophetic edge that can enable you to believe for a similar thing to happen in your life. What are you praying for and believing for right now? Perhaps one of the testimonies that I have shared can release a prophetic word in your life regarding these situations, opening up a new door for God to move and work in your life, and bringing you into an uncommon result that otherwise might not have happened.

Pray and ask God to bring this prophetic edge to your life right now, and to release kingdom power and authority in a new realm that will begin to solve your problem, situation, or circumstances as you trust God to create perhaps an uncommon answer that is different than anything you have previously heard or seen from anyone else, yet it brings needed relief for you right now. I believe this will be the start for a continuation of uncommon strategies and uncommon answers that at times may really be weird and unique, yet filled with solutions and answers in every realm that you need it.

Kris Vallotton, who is on staff at Bethel Church in Redding, California, asked this question in his book, *Heavy Rain*: "What would your city look like if the Kingdom of God were superimposed over every realm of society?"[9] Now think about that same thought and apply it to your family, your job, and your church. Jot down some notes here to help you remember, so that you can return to pray about these thoughts in the future.

Chapter Six

Tolerated, Appreciated, Celebrated

WHAT are you appreciated and celebrated for? Do you even know? Knowing this is helpful as you learn, develop, and walk in the gifts and strengths that the Lord has given you. The word *appreciate* means more than just being thankful; it also has the definition "to go up in value." When something appreciates, it is worth more later on than when you started or when it was acquired. First Peter 4:10 reveals this truth: "As each one has received a gift, minister it to one another, as good stewards of the manifold grace of God." Each and every believer has received at least one gift, and probably a whole lot more according to other Scripture verses that we will not explore presently.

The purpose of the gift is to share it with others. Unlike some gifts in the natural that are just intended for your own personal use, such as a new set of golf clubs or a bottle of perfume, these spiritual gifts are given so that others can also be blessed and ultimately appreciated and celebrated too.

There really are three sets of gifts in the Bible, including the ones detailed in Romans 12, which are specific gifts of the Father; 1 Corinthians 12, which are given by the Holy Spirit; and then in Ephesians 4, the five specific gifts given by Jesus. But in the passage above from 1 Peter, we are informed that we are to be good stewards of these gifts, and in 1 Corinthians 4:2 the Bible says that the requirement of stewards is faithfulness.

Key # 1: Be faithful.

About eight years prior to the writing of this book, I read a book by Dutch Sheets called *Intercessory Prayer*, and somewhere in the first couple of chapters, Dutch made a suggestion about the Lord's Prayer that went something like this: When you pray the Lord's Prayer, and you say, "Thy kingdom come, Thy will be done," believe that it happens now, as opposed to sometime in the future. When I read that silently sitting in the chair in my living room, I replied out loud, "I can do that." It was a specific download from heaven directly to me that began to change the course of my ministry.

Two weeks later I was ministering as a guest at a local church, and there was a lady who came up for prayer because her knee would click out loud whenever she would walk. If you were nearby, you could hear it click loud and clear. I had her walk across the platform at the church, all the while proclaiming, "Thy kingdom come, Thy will be done," believing that the click would go away as I prayed those prayers. The third time across the platform, the click disappeared and never returned. Now, isn't that amazing? Everyone saw it, or I guess I should say, everyone heard it or maybe they didn't hear it, and I guess they didn't see it either, but whatever, you get the picture, or maybe not. Hmm … That was a strange sentence, wasn't it? But I am going to leave it.

What happened? God healed her as I took the truth of Dutch Sheets's teaching suggestion and put it into practice. As a result, that launched a more deliberate and intentional healing ministry that I am now known for both in our area geographically and somewhat in other places across the country. What has happened is that the healing ministry is but one of several areas that people appreciate and perhaps even celebrate about me. It has helped define my ministry and enabled me to see a broader spectrum of the kingdom because of it. God has used my faith to help me get into doors that otherwise might have remained closed.

In the previous chapter, I wrote about the race between the rabbit, squirrel, and the duck, how they were all celebrated and appreciated in their differences, and how they were uncommon in their gifting. The Bible says it is not good to compare ourselves with others. I know of many people who have approached me and asked me to pray an anointing over them so that they could have a healing ministry too. Normally, I decline.

First, it is not a task to be taken lightly. Second, these gifts are not from me but from God. I believe we can pray and ask for them, but He still gives the gifts. As I stated before, I don't really operate in the gift of healing, but rather in the gift of faith. It was the gift of faith that was in operation when I read the book and responded, "I can do that."

Third, often when people want a gift so easily transferred to them, there are character issues that need to be examined and worked on too. Working in and for the kingdom is work, and while very enjoyable, it is still work. Believers who desire certain things need to understand that. We cannot tolerate lazy Christians. I know that some will disagree with me here, but if and when they write their own books, they can share why. Bill Johnson was quoted as saying, "What we tolerate will dominate." I have met a lot of lazy Christians over the years who think they are entitled to all sorts of free stuff and that as children of God, they can just sit back and have everything given to them. But we need to remember that we are on a battleship, not a cruise line, as John Wimber once stated.

First Timothy tells us that we are to be good soldiers. Paul talks in Ephesians about the Christian vocation, not the Christian vacation. It takes work in prayer, study, seeking after God, avoiding the appearance of evil, walking in integrity, flowing with and hearing the voice of the Holy Spirit, and then being ready at a moment's notice to change direction and yield to what God is telling us to do even though we may have felt led to study and prepare in a different direction.

Key # 2: It's a vocation, not a vacation.

Sometimes people ask me to pray for a double-portion anointing on them, and to be honest, I just don't think that exists in the New Testament. Yes, Elisha asked for a double portion from Elijah, and he received it, but first sons in the Old Testament were given a double portion. Yet, in the New Testament, we are told that while faith comes in a measure, according to Romans 12, the anointing comes without measure, as was written about Jesus in John 3:34.

Faith comes with a measure. Faith comes with a measure. Bet you thought that was a misprint, didn't you? But I am emphasizing it for a reason. If something has a measure to it, you can then double it, but if there is no way to measure it, how can you double it? The Holy Spirit is given without measure. I can't even see the Holy Spirit, so how can I measure Him, and then double Him? The Holy Spirit and the anointing are the same. You might say, "Well, how can you see faith?" The Bible says in Hebrews 11:1 that faith is a substance—and I can see substances—but it goes on to say that it is the evidence of things not seen. It did not say that faith is not seen, but rather faith is the evidence of *things* not seen. Things! Things! Things! These are things that have not been seen yet, but will soon be seen because the substance of faith is growing, enlarging, and embarking on a journey that will produce a harvest or a yield that will release and reveal those things that you are believing for to become a reality. Faith is a substance, so it can be doubled, tripled, or multiplied greatly; but the Spirit is given without measure.

If you have a glass of water with exactly 12 ounces of fluid in it, you can double it to 24 ounces and then double it again to 48 ounces. If you have 2 bricks in the yard, you can double them to 4 bricks and then to 8, then 16, then 32, 64, 128, 256, 512, 1024, 2048, 4096, and so on it goes—and that would be a lot of bricks. But can you double the amount of air that is in your house right now? No, but you are just glad that there is more than enough for you and everyone else. The same is true with the Holy Spirit, as there is always enough for everyone, for every situation, in every circumstance, with every need, and for everybody. The anointing and the Holy Spirit are limitless, so instead of doubling it, I just ask for more, because I know there is more.

Before we shift gears, I want to share another verse, this one from Colossians 1:25. Paul is speaking and he says, "I became a minister according to the stewardship from God, which was given to me, for you, to fulfill the word of God." I love this Scripture because it so keenly ties up the gifts in a nice package and demonstrates to us whom the gifts are from, whom they are for, and what the reason is as well. Let's break it down and unpack it just a bit.

Paul is a minister. That is a given. But you are too! If you are a believer in Jesus, then you are a minister of the Gospel of Jesus. Some of you might be thinking that the ministers are the paid staff workers at your church, and while that may be true in title and theory, the reality of the Bible is that every believer is also a minister. Paul goes on to say that he is a minister according to the stewardship from God. Remember what we wrote above about the requirement of stewards, according to 1 Corinthians 4:2? They are to be faithful. And God is always faithful, even when we are not. Very cool!

Then the verse clearly identifies that the gift of this ministry is given to me, for you. Stop and say this out loud right now: "To me, for you." Say it again. And again. And again. Get it down in your spirit that these gifts and callings from God are given to all of us for the good of others.

It doesn't stop there, but it goes on to accentuate that the primary purpose is to fulfill the word of God. Everything we do needs to have as its aim fulfilling the word of God and expanding the kingdom in a way that will promote Jesus and further His cause. Whether that be bake sales or Christmas pageants, youth groups or mission trips, discipleship classes or prayer circles, we always need to be about our Father's business and to do only what we see Him doing, according to John 5:19.

Ministry comes in many shapes, sizes, and specifications, and I am okay with that, as long as it is designed, defined, and deployed by the Holy Spirit. That was a good sentence. How about an Amen!

Key #3: The gifts for me are for you.

Let's move away from healing faith for awhile and shift into another realm of faith: faith for everyday situations and opportunities. I believe it will further our understanding of the title of this chapter and of this book too.

In 1993, we moved from Houston, Texas, to Hugoton, Kansas. In Houston I had been on staff at a Lutheran church that was known—and sometimes tolerated, but mostly appreciated—for being a church that believed in the power of God and the gifts of the Spirit as being for today. On many occasions it was also celebrated. This happened at that church because, years before I ever met him, the senior pastor had an encounter with the Holy Spirit and positioned himself to walk out that encounter in a powerful way. It was not always easy, but it sure was fun.

When we moved to Hugoton, Kansas, my new position was that of senior pastor for a small remnant of folks who had encountered the Holy Spirit in another local rural church and had planted this one. This was indeed a challenge for this suburban guy who loved the suburban lifestyle, but after a couple of years, I found out that there really is more than one way to skin a cat. And like John Osteen used to say, "If the cat doesn't like it, let the cat turn around." I began to turn around.

Meanwhile, back on the farm in Houston, while living in the suburbs, we had purchased some land from our pastor who lived out on a farm about twenty-five minutes from the church. As I recall, he had a five-acre tract of land that was part of a larger farm that one of our elders owned and had subdivided into a group of smaller tracts for believers to come out and live in the country with good neighbors. We thought it would be fun to live out there someday, so we purchased one acre for $5000 and began to cultivate the land. Our pastor sold us the land because he needed some extra cash to finish the house he was building on his property.

We brought in a utility pole and put in some underground water pipes to the nearest neighbor to use water off of his well, strategically planted a bunch of pine trees and oak trees, had some dirt brought in for two berms to create some landscape design where our driveway would eventually go, and just enjoyed being out there when we could. When we discovered we would be going to Kansas, we listed the land with a "for sale by owner" sign and our Kansas phone number, hoping that someone else would pick up on our vision, but no one ever did.

Now fast forward about two years. I was praying in Kansas one day, and the Lord spoke to me and told me to give the land away. We prayed and felt good about it, so we set out on a journey to give the land away, believing that we were yielding to the voice of God. You might say, "Wow, that was generous and would require a lot of faith!" Well, it did, but we had a track record at that time of giving away cars, appliances, and larger sums of money. Such testimonies have been shared in previous chapters, and others are listed in my first book. So this was not something really new to us.

We put the word out and intentionally asked a nonprofit group in Houston if they would like to have it. They responded that they indeed would like to have it, so we made plans to go to Houston to sign the papers, mow the property, and clean it up before the sale. I then made plane reservations to go the weekend before Father's Day, and all three of us would fly there, including my wife Diane and our son Jason, who was about four years old at the time.

A week or two after I made the plane reservations, the Lord spoke to me and told me to delay the trip one week. I yielded to that, but with some reservation, because I knew that most of the time, when you change your airline tickets, you also receive an imposed penalty for doing such a thing. But the Lord assured me it would work out, so I called the airline, and it was offering a limited special for folks who might want to change their plans without any additional fees. That was a blessing! I then contacted a few friends in Houston and told them we would be coming a week later. Soon after that a local pastor called me and asked me if I could preach for him on that specific Sunday we would be in town because he was going to be out of town for a wedding, so I agreed to fill in for him.

When we finally arrived in Houston, we went out to work on the property and took down the "for sale" sign because we anticipated giving it to this nonprofit ministry. As we were working on the land, a friend of ours who lived out there too came over for a visit and inquired why we were there, as he knew we now lived in Kansas. I explained to him that we were cleaning up the land and planned to give it away to this nonprofit. He soon excused himself and said he would be back in a little while. Then the unexpected began to happen.

I received a phone call from the nonprofit group and they had changed their minds and did not want to receive our generous gift. They basically declined, stating they did not want to get stuck with the taxes in case they could not sell it. Their thought was that we had it listed for three years and it did not sell, so they did not want to get in the same predicament. I tried to challenge them and say that they could have listed it for a lot less than what we had it listed for, but the decision had been made.

I began to wonder why we had spent all of this money to fly down there to make this transaction, only to have it fall apart. Soon after, the neighbor who had stopped by earlier returned and made the following offer: He wanted to buy our land for our original asking price, and then deed the land as a donation back to the church, which in turn would deed it back to our former pastor, as he always really wanted the land. My initial thought was that God told us to give the land away, and I shared that with him, but he replied that maybe God would allow us to give the money away instead.

So we prayed about it for a bit and felt good about this new option and that God was in it. We made the verbal agreement and signed all of the necessary papers later during that trip. The weird thing about this is that my property was kind of in the middle of a dirt road that ultimately came to a dead end, and this friend drove past my "for sale" sign for three years and never once offered to buy it. Yet, on the exact day we were there to make a transaction with this nonprofit organization that had now fallen through, he came over and made this amazing offer.

There are several more pieces to this amazing story that need to be shared. First of all, the friend who purchased the land worked for a major oil company, and the week prior when we originally were going to come down to Houston, he was in a foreign country working on oil exploration and would have missed us altogether, so God knew that we needed to change our plans.

You may remember that I was invited to speak at a local church, so I went and did that on Sunday, and two more wonderful things happened. The love offering that morning covered all of our traveling expenses to Houston, including our airfare, rental car, hotel, and food. And there was a Hispanic pastor in the service that morning who invited me to come and be a guest the very next day on TBN there in Houston, so I did two shows with translation that were aired over most of Texas, Florida, and Central and South America. Wow, what a blessing! By simply yielding to God and changing our plans to come to Houston on another weekend, all of these incredible things happened in a timely sequence that only God could have orchestrated. Similar to our plans regarding the Holiday Bowl in a previous chapter, as we listened to God, and yielded to His design and plan for our lives, we also received a yield in return, only this time we had over $5,000 to give away.

The actual transaction of the land sale with the mailed arrival of the check took several more weeks, but it arrived in a very timely way, so our journey of giving money away to bless others began. I was scheduled to go and minister in the San Antonio area and also attend a conference. I had a pastor friend who wanted to link up for dinner while I was there and asked me if he could bring a friend. It turned out that he and his wife brought a young lady in his congregation to dinner. I soon learned why.

She had recently broken up with her boyfriend of many years, lost her job, was about to be evicted from her apartment, was suicidal, and had nowhere to go or live. During our conversation, I asked her how much her rent and any penalties might be, and she said she needed $400 to stay there another month. Can you see God smiling on this situation? Not only was I thankful and appreciating God giving me all of this money to give away, but God was making this situation "appreciate" and go up in value. It has been said that what God initiates He appreciates, and in my life that normally means what He initiates then goes up in value and is worth more when He has completed it.

I was so happy and blessed to give the first $400 of the $5000 away to this young lady to help her in her time of need. I did make the check out to the pastor, and he paid the rent. I later heard from the pastor that this one event totally changed her perspective in that she got a better job, new friends, and was no longer suicidal. God knew it all, but I had to yield the whole way through, and then He brought back so many more yields to my life and the lives of others as we gave and gave and gave and helped so many other people and ministries receive their harvest too. For this young lady, she rededicated her life to Jesus and was on a new path.

Proverbs 3:5–6 beautifully describe these actions: "Trust in the Lord with all your heart, and lean not on your own understanding. In all your ways acknowledge Him, and He shall direct your paths." That is exactly what happened. In the natural, it made no sense to try to give away some land or change my dates of travel, but God knew that if I leaned into His ways and His mode of operation, that He would direct my paths, and everything would turn out great! It happened!

Let me add two verses from Proverbs 4:26–27, from which I have a teaching message titled "Avoiding Pathetic Pathology": "Ponder the path of your feet, and let all your ways be established. Do not turn to the right or the left, remove your foot from evil." These are great and precious words from the Bible for us today. We need to ponder the path of our feet. In this message, I took several words that had the root word *path* in them and wrote and shared the message. The five words were sympathy, empathy, pathetic, pathology, and apathy. I won't re-teach that message here, as it would take up too much space, but you can order it from me using the contact information in the back of the book.

When Mary received the word from the Lord that she would conceive and give birth to the Savior of the world, she pondered those things in her heart. Proverbs 4 suggests that we should ponder the path of our feet. As you do that and pray and trust God, I believe you can move from being tolerated to appreciated to ultimately being celebrated as you walk on the path God has for you.

My path includes many areas of ministry where extra faith is needed. Yours might be one of mercy, sharing hope, or being very prophetic. Remember, your gift is to be stewarded with faithfulness and then shared with others. Your position in the kingdom is to yield to God and then bless and encourage others, thus advancing the kingdom of God in your sphere of influence.

I want to be faithful with what God has given me, and part of doing this includes writing books and articles. Someday, when I get to heaven, I expect to hear these words in a commending and kind way: "Well done, thou good and faithful servant." I don't want to just hear the first word as a question: "Well?" "Well …" or even, "Well, well, well." One of the best things that I can hope to experience as I enter into heaven someday is to hear God call me one who was faithful. What a tremendous blessing and encouraging thought that is!

I think you are probably in agreement with me too. So let's move to the Journey section now with anticipation, eagerness, and expectation of how God may want to mold and position us for a great yield in the future.

Journey

If you own your house, collectibles, and even stocks, you want them to appreciate in value over time. And as that hopefully happens, you will appreciate that you made the investment, which ultimately will culminate in some sort of celebration when you reap the harvest and increase of that investment. The same principal applies to you as a member of the body of Christ and the family of God. God thought you were so valuable that He was willing to die for you and yes, even so valuable that He was willing to live for you too.

I'm sure you have made mistakes; we all have. But for those who repent, God is faithful and just to forgive us all of our sins and remove our transgressions from us, cleansing us from all unrighteousness. God is so faithful, and we are created in His image, so that faithfulness is like a spiritual inheritance that is given to us as a part of the victory in the cross of Jesus and His resurrection. We can rely on Jesus to help us, encourage us, and bless us with everything we need that pertains to life and godliness, including the area and realm of faithfulness.

Take a moment right now to repent of any action or any times when you have not been faithful, and then begin to thank God that He is so faithful. Don't tolerate unfaithful acts or mediocrity in the Kingdom of God. Remember, even if you mess up, His faithfulness is new every morning. This is a new day, and as you have just read this chapter, you too can believe God for great and wonderful things, and for His plan to be implemented on the path that you are walking on. He loves you and will work with you, and He won't give up on you. Others may have given up on you, but in God's eyes, you are appreciated and being celebrated right now. How do I know this? The Bible says that all of heaven rejoices and celebrates when one person repents. If you just repented, there is a celebration happening in heaven right now that will outdo, outlast, and outshine any party you have ever seen or heard of on earth.

Key # 4: Appreciation leads to celebration

Everything of value has something worth celebrating. As you read this book, I believe that your value for the kingdom is increasing. And as your value increases, so does the appreciation value as well.

God is amazing! And so are you. Remember, you were created in His image. So you are amazing too.

Chapter Seven

Study Time: Part 3

IN the conclusion of our previous "Study Time" in Chapter 4, I wrote in the Journey section about moving past negative thought patterns that could create barriers in your walk with the Lord. Earlier today as I was writing on Facebook, I posted the following quote by Bill Johnson: "You won't have to watch what you say if you watch what you think." I wonder what would have happened with Saul's daughter (aka King David's wife) had she followed that advice.

Notice the emphasis in the following passages:

- "The wicked in his proud countenance does not seek God; God is in none of his **thoughts**" (Psalm 10:4).
- "All day they twist my words; all their **thoughts** are against me for evil" (Psalm 56:5).
- "The **thoughts** of the wicked are an abomination to the Lord" (Proverbs 15:26a).
- "'For My **thoughts** are not your **thoughts**, nor are your ways My ways,' says the Lord" (Isaiah 55:8).
- "O Jerusalem, wash your heart from wickedness, that you may be saved. How long shall your evil **thoughts** lodge within you?" (Jeremiah 4:14).

What I hear God saying in these verses is that He wants us to yield our thoughts to Him. His desire is to bring a larger yield into our lives, if we can trust Him with our thought lives too. Let's look at some more verses with wonderful promises and life-giving words regarding our thoughts.

- "For I know the **thoughts** that I think toward you, says the Lord, **thoughts** of peace and not of evil, to give you a future and a hope" (Jeremiah 29:11).
- "How precious also are Your **thoughts** to me, O God! How great is the sum of them!" (Psalm 139:17).
- "Commit your works to the Lord, and your **thoughts** will be established" (Proverbs 16:3).
- "For as the heavens are higher than the earth, so are My ways higher than your ways, and My **thoughts** than your **thoughts**" (Isaiah 55:9).
- "I **thought** about my ways, and turned my feet to Your testimonies" (Psalm 119:59).

As I am writing this, I just prepared and shared a recent message from Revelation 19:10, which says, "The testimony of Jesus is the spirit of prophecy." In other words, when you listen to a testimony, don't just nod your head in agreement with the person who is sharing. Let the positive words of that testimony release a prophetic thought in you for a word of knowledge, a prophetic word, or some wisdom and discernment to be loosed in your life to bring you an answer or a miraculous process so that the testimony that you just heard actually releases and expands the kingdom of God in you. This will create a domino effect and promote the life of Jesus in someone else too.

Now, tie that in with the verse above from Psalm 119:59. As our thoughts turn away from evil and toward God and His testimonies, then even those testimonies can and should release a prophetic word in you. What am I saying? If we yield our thoughts to God, He will direct our steps on the path and begin to change problems into solutions with a greater yield than we have experienced in the past, simply because we took the thoughts captive to the obedience of Christ. That obedience enables you to occupy and enjoy the land. Remember, one of the premise verses at the very beginning of this book, Isaiah 1:19, says, "If you are willing and obedient, you will eat the good of the land."

What would have happened if Michal had yielded her thoughts to the Lord? Would she have reproduced new life? I believe she would have, and the story would have been much different. In fact, much like the movie *Back to the Future* (in which, when certain events were changed, pictures faded in and out of previous newspaper articles), certain events later on in David's life may also have been much different.

Mini-Journey

What thoughts can you begin to change right now that will ultimately begin to change your future? Seriously, think about it. Stop and pray, asking God to reveal thoughts that promote action that is flowing against the river of the Holy Spirit that inhibit your spiritual growth and takes precedence over Jesus. This really is important.

* * *

You may remember that King David basically said he was going to be less prideful with his reply to Michal, "I will be even more undignified than this." How does pride manifest? Let me give you some examples:

A proud look! You smugly look at someone in church and just smile in that peculiar way that lets others know you think you are better than them. Or perhaps, it is that look you give the driver in traffic who just cut you off. As a beautiful, wonderfully saved Christian with a Jesus fish on the back of your car, you would never resort to any hand gestures, but that look—you know what I mean. I see you smiling even now because you recognize the truth in this paragraph.

How about pointing your fingers at things that happen in church or whispering to your friends about what happened while in the foyer after the service. So many people want the presence of God without His manifestations. Some of you reading this may have had some initial escape thoughts with the first chapter and the story from Diane and Harris in Minnesota. If you are still reading, I commend you. The manifestations just lead us to Jesus. The word *manifestation* obviously comes from the word *manifest*, and the word *manifest* means to make known, to reveal, and to become conspicuous. God uses manifestations of various forms and shapes both in the natural and supernatural realm to reveal Himself to others and to make His Kingdom known so that you and I become so conspicuous with His presence that it is nearly impossible for others to miss and neither see nor experience what God is doing. It is like a huge spotlight shining down on us to reveal what God is up to. It is His way of externalizing and exteriorizing His incarnate and divine personification to us. (That may be a new Jayism sentence.)

David's dancing was a manifestation. Shaking, swaying, or falling under the power of God is a manifestation. Sharing or receiving a prophetic word is a manifestation, as is experiencing healing in your body or seeing someone else get well through prayer and perhaps an impartation through the laying on of hands, according to Mark 16. I will discuss falling under the power of God in a later chapter so that those who don't have a clear grasp of it will gain some understanding. I believe that demonstration with explanation brings edification. I don't want anyone confused in any way, so I will later explain this so that edification (the building up of your faith) can be increased in your life.

First Corinthians 12:6–8 reports this: "And there are diversities of activities, but it is the same God who works all in all. But the manifestation of the Spirit is given to each one for the profit of all: for to one is given the word of wisdom through the Spirit, to another the word of knowledge through the same Spirit."

When the verse above says "for the profit of all," that means for the profit of everyone in the kingdom and all who are nearby who are about to enter the kingdom as they experience the manifestations. Those manifestations draw them in for a closer look to see who this Jesus really is. If they yield to the Holy Spirit, then they receive a yield in return.

I like what 2 Corinthians 4:1–3 emphasizes:

> Therefore, since we have this ministry, as we have received mercy, we do not lose heart. But we have renounced the hidden things of shame, not walking in craftiness nor handling the word of God deceitfully, but by manifestation of the truth commending ourselves to every man's conscience in the sight of God. But even if our gospel is veiled, it is veiled to those who are perishing.

Notice what I previously emphasized: You have this ministry. Isn't that cool? And as you repent, get rid of evil and destructive thoughts, and pull down strongholds, you are no longer walking in your own strength or plans and purposes but now the plans and purposes of God. Yes, there is even a manifestation of the truth, and you can use that truth to commend yourself. Sounds like it borders on pride, but God is using this confession from your mouth to authenticate your thoughts and display His righteousness. The Bible says in Psalm 107:2, "Let the redeemed of the Lord say so."

But if you stop talking and sharing, then the Gospel becomes veiled or hidden to those who are lost. So when you are following Jesus and He challenges to you to share, offer to pray with someone, give someone a financial blessing, or just extend a helpful hand, those are also supernatural times of manifestations. If you are following John 5:19 and, like Jesus, are only doing what you see the Father doing, then you will be flowing in the supernatural. Keep in mind that the supernatural is the natural to God.

Pride will prevent you from yielding. Pride whispers in your ear that what God is asking you to do is beneath you. I think that is probably some of what happened to Michal. She was the daughter of a king and now the wife of a king, and she had only known the royalty side of things all her life. Her new husband was down there dancing on the street, acting like a common person, and she could not allow herself to be lowered to that level. It was, after all, undignified. What would the people think? She might lose her authority if they thought she was like one of them.

If only she had taken those thoughts captive and responded like David did, who recognized that there was a higher King than even himself. David danced and danced and danced, and Michal fumed and fumed and fumed. Who do you think had the most fun? Who got in the presence of God and who moved even farther away from the presence of God? Who got to experience life and who was then barren in life?

Let me tell you a story. Back in our second year of marriage, we were living in a very nice apartment in Houston that was very tropical and had some nice pools and recreation areas. Diane and I had one of the rare fights that we have had in our thirty-four years of marriage. I suspect we've had less than one a year. But this one was a gangbuster, and I remember shouting as I went out the door that I was going to go some place a long way away from her. Of course, I slammed the door for emphasis, took one step, and sat down. I stayed there for quite awhile too. You see, I was lying to myself and to her. I have always loved being with Diane, and hate it even when I have to travel in ministry and be gone for any length of time. I can't wait to get home and share with my best friend all that God was doing or had done. Moving out of her presence was absolutely not anything I would want to do.

The same is true with God. I just love being in His presence, and in His presence things happen that can't happen anywhere else. The miraculous is available at a moment's notice, and His power is so real and so tangible. I've seen so many people come forward for prayer, longing to get me or some member of my team to pray for them, only to get well and announce it to everyone before anyone even had a chance to pray for them.

I remember one time in Des Moines, after teaching the Word, I was explaining the procedures of the healing emphasis ministry time that was coming up and also sharing some of the manifestations that might occur, when suddenly a man in the second row jumped up, shouted that his knee stopped hurting, and began to run around the worship center. I had never met him and could not verify his story, but the pastor assured me that this man had been limping for a long time and could not possibly run like that. Every time I returned to this church, he would approach me and remind me of that night and share with me that he was still well. The guy simply got in God's presence and was healed instantly.

Recently in Omaha, at a local Lutheran church where I have previously led quarterly healing services, I was praying for people in the front who had pain in various places, and I could see one lady off to the right side who was moving her neck back and forth. I simply stopped praying and asked her what was happening, and she told me and everyone who was there that she came to church with tremendous pain in her neck, which she had been experiencing for a very long time. Then, so quickly while standing up in front, the pain just disappeared. What happened? She got in the presence of God and was touched without anyone praying for her. That is simply amazing. Healing is available in His presence, but so are forgiveness and righteousness. Read on.

First Thessalonians 3:6–13 in the New International Version gives us these words and this blessing:

> But Timothy has just now come to us from you and has brought good news about your faith and love. He has told us that you always have pleasant memories of us and that you long to see us, just as we also

Study Time: Part 3

long to see you. Therefore, brothers and sisters, in all our distress and persecution we were encouraged about you because of your faith. For now we really live, since you are standing firm in the Lord. How can we thank God enough for you in return for all the joy we have in the presence of our God because of you? Night and day we pray most earnestly that we may see you again and supply what is lacking in your faith. Now may our God and Father himself and our Lord Jesus clear the way for us to come to you. May the Lord make your love increase and overflow for each other and for everyone else, just as ours does for you. May he strengthen your hearts so that you will be blameless and holy in the presence of our God and Father when our Lord Jesus comes with all his holy ones.

I like where it says, "Now we really live." How does this happen? By being in His presence. Then Paul goes on to share about the joy that Christians have by being in the presence of God. Somebody shout JOY! Gotta Have IT. JOY! Really Need IT. JOY! There's Power in IT. JOY! Let Me Have IT.

Then another blessing is being blameless and holy in the presence of God. This is so wonderful. You know what I mean. You've been there. You've experienced this. After repenting and being honest with God, as He cleansed you with His Word, washed away your sins, and removed all of your transgressions far from you, you experienced true joy, refreshing, and the wonder of being blameless and holy in His sight.

In Psalm 51:1–17 David is crying out for this very thing to happen to him. Read these impacting words from David's heart:

Have mercy upon me, O God,
According to Your lovingkindness;
According to the multitude of Your tender mercies,
Blot out my transgressions.
Wash me thoroughly from my iniquity,
And cleanse me from my sin.
For I acknowledge my transgressions,
And my sin is always before me.
Against You, You only, have I sinned,
And done this evil in Your sight—

That You may be found just when You speak,
And blameless when You judge.
Behold, I was brought forth in iniquity,
And in sin my mother conceived me.
Behold, You desire truth in the inward parts,
And in the hidden part You will make me to know wisdom.
Purge me with hyssop, and I shall be clean;
Wash me, and I shall be whiter than snow.
Make me hear joy and gladness,
That the bones You have broken may rejoice.
Hide Your face from my sins,
And blot out all my iniquities.
Create in me a clean heart, O God,
And renew a steadfast spirit within me.
Do not cast me away from Your presence,
And do not take Your Holy Spirit from me.
Restore to me the joy of Your salvation,
And uphold me by Your generous Spirit.
Then I will teach transgressors Your ways,
And sinners shall be converted to You.
Deliver me from the guilt of bloodshed, O God,
The God of my salvation,
And my tongue shall sing aloud of Your righteousness.
O Lord, open my lips,
And my mouth shall show forth Your praise.
For You do not desire sacrifice, or else I would give it;
You do not delight in burnt offering.
The sacrifices of God are a broken spirit,
A broken and a contrite heart—
These, O God, You will not despise.

All of these things are manifestations of God's grace and love in our lives. Who wouldn't want to experience this? Again, good theology without experience of theophany would be an utter waste of time. God says all things are possible if you will just get in My presence. God responds with forgiving eyes and a longing heart to retrieve and receive those who have strayed away, with open arms of receptivity. He is not sitting in heaven with a heavy hand and a big rod to whip us into shape. No, His hands are open to receive us with forgiveness, grace, and faithfulness that go way beyond anything we could ever imagine.

I love the kind and generous words of Acts 3:19: "Repent therefore and be converted, that your sins may be blotted out, so that times of refreshing may come from the presence of the Lord." We understand *repent* to mean simply to turn around 180 degrees and go the opposite direction. We know that as we do that, our sins are blotted out and totally removed from us. God will never bring them up again. The Bible clearly states in Romans that there is no condemnation to those who are in Christ Jesus. Once you have been forgiven, it's like it never happened. And then those glorious times of refreshing come from being in His presence. It really is indescribable. To even try would be futile, so I won't; but if you have participated in this verse, then you know what I am writing and sharing about.

I also want you see that word *converted*, as it is a word that describes something that moves from one position to another, or is in one form and then takes on a different shape. Think of a couch that opens up to a convertible sofa. Or a car on which the top disappears with the push of a button and then you are driving a convertible. Perhaps you have seen the large transformers on power poles, and there are electric lines going in one side and out the other. I've been told that the power in one line is converted into another power design on the other side due to the conversion in the transformer.

Romans 12 instructs us to be transformed by the renewing of our minds. There are those *thoughts* again. But there is a power exchange on the electric poles with the transformers, and there is a power exchange in the words of Acts 3:19 when we move from our own realm of sin, wrong thinking, and barriers that prevent the benefits of the presence of God from being released to a new power realm in which just being in His presence can cause amazing, miraculous, and fantastic things to happen.

Deuteronomy 4:36–38 gives us a glimpse of this:

> Out of heaven He let you hear His voice, that He might instruct you; on earth He showed you His great fire, and you heard His words out of the midst of the fire. And because He loved your fathers, therefore He chose their descendants after them; and He brought you out of Egypt with His Presence, with His mighty power, driving out from before you nations

greater and mightier than you, to bring you in, to give you their land as an inheritance, as it is this day.

Notice, it says they came out with His presence and His mighty power. The children were in one condition in Egypt as slaves, but as they came out, it was like going through a transformer, and they were in the process of being changed to that of being free.

There is a direct connection and correlation between being in His presence and operating in His power. Remember, I previously shared and taught about power and authority. But releasing power and authority in you and walking in His presence and power is a radical step beyond what most believers will ever experience. Why? Because they don't want to yield, which is entirely the reason it took forty years to reach the Promised Land. The children of Israel simply did not want to yield to God.

Part of what I am going to share with you now I learned from Pastor James Bradley from Family Worship Center in Kokomo, Indiana, when he was a guest at the church we attend in Omaha. Some of it is additional information (or rather, *transformation*) that I studied out as well.

In Deuteronomy 33:15, the Bible tells us this: "Your sandals shall be iron and bronze: As your days, so shall your strength be." Speaking of the children of Israel, God was saying that their shoes were tough enough for the trip. Most biblical scholars would agree that when the children of Israel were slaves in Egypt, they wore some sort of shoes and protective covering on their feet when making the bricks out of clay and straw, but when a slave was taken in the public realm, his shoes were probably removed as a sign that he or she was a slave. Thus, being barefooted distinguished them from those who were free at the time.

When Moses told the children of Israel to get ready to move out of Egypt, he told them to get their shoes. This was a new thought because they did not wear shoes in public, but this was the beginning of the conversion and transforming process, moving from one form to another for these people. As they traveled in the wilderness we are told in Nehemiah 9:21 that God would sustain them in their shoes, and that the shoes would never wear out. This is a very interesting point and must be examined a bit closer.

If you are a lady reading this or you are a man who has a wife or a girlfriend, let me ask this question: How many shoes do you have, or how many shoes does your wife or girlfriend have? Let me just say, I have never met any lady in America who had only one pair of shoes and was satisfied with a limited number of shoes. When I ask this question in a group, I sometimes find ladies who have upwards of fifty pairs of shoes. So while God sustained them with one pair of shoes, it certainly was not a prosperous position.

The same can be shared about the men who are reading this. Most men do not want to have the same meal over and over and over and over again. But these people were sustained on manna, which means, "What is it?" We attend a large and growing multicultural church, and my African American brothers would say, "What it is." However you slice it, "what is it" or "what it is," they probably boiled, baked, breaded, basted, grilled, and fried that manna, yet it certainly was not a prosperous meal time for forty looooooon nnnnnnnnnnnnnngggggggggggggggg years. "Honey, can't you make it taste any different?" Boring. Sustaining? Yes. Prospering? No.

Finally as the children of Israel were about to go into the Promised Land, Joshua told the people in Joshua 1:3, "Every place that the sole of your foot shall tread upon, [the LORD has] given you." I want you to catch this important conversion. When the children were in public in Egypt, they did not wear any shoes, which presented them to the general population as slaves and not free. Then they put on their shoes to go out into the public to travel to the Promised Land, and the shoes did not wear out.

But now they were about to go into the Promised Land, and once again they were to take off their shoes. Why? Because now the conversion is happening. Now the transformation is about to take place. This is to signal that they were finally moving from being in slave mentality (which they inherited from their parents who died in the wilderness) to being actual landowners.

WOW, DID YOU CATCH THAT? LANDOWNERS! This is an awesome thing that the Lord was doing for these people. For hundreds of years, the ancestors of those who were now entering in had only been recognized as slaves, but now in their freedom, they were being transformed into Promised Land owners.

In Ephesians 6, as a part of our new identity in Christ, we are to put on the whole armor of God, including placing on our feet the Gospel of peace. We are to take the peace of God to those in conflict and those warring in their hearts, helping them see and experience a new life, a converted life, in

Jesus by experiencing the very presence of God in their hearts, minds, and lives. Those that don't know Jesus are slaves to the flesh and to the world, but as they discover who they are in Jesus and put on those new shoes, they also become spiritual landowners of the kingdom of God, here on earth just like it is in heaven.

And as we all go together along this new path, we soon discover what a joy, wonder, and privilege it is to be on the same path with Jesus. It is everything David was crying out for in Psalm 51, everything that Michal needed, and everything that we can experience just by getting into the very presence of God.

In conclusion, read these verses and let them promote the next step of your journey with God that will add so much to your life. It will amaze you as you literally see yourself being converted into something entirely different, wonderful, incredible, and optional because you have yielded to it.

"You will show me the path of life; In Your presence is fullness of joy; At Your right hand are pleasures forevermore," as written in Psalm 16:11. Acts 2:28 takes it further with these words: "You have made known to me the ways of life; You will make me full of joy in Your presence." And 1 Thessalonians 2:19 takes us even further with this same theme: "For what is our hope, or joy, or crown of rejoicing? Is it not even you in the presence of our Lord Jesus Christ at His coming?" Finally, Jude 1:24 is a great conclusion: "Now to Him who is able to keep you from stumbling, And to present you faultless before the presence of His glory with exceeding joy."

Journey

There was a lot in that chapter, wasn't there? As I completed writing it, I kind of had to catch my breath. Maybe you feel the same way. So let's just pause, slow down a bit, and rest. Close your eyes for a moment and just meditate on what it means to get into the presence of God. As you have your eyes closed, ask God to reveal Himself to you and to show you His conversion power with which He wants to transform you. Take a moment right now to relax, close your eyes, and spend a few minutes alone with God, in His presence.

When you are finished, write down your experience. Remind yourself of your theophany so that you can do this again in the near future and become a spiritual landowner. Now you can experience true times of refreshing from the presence of the Lord, on your own land. Please don't just read through this without actually stopping for a few minutes. Just rest in His presence and let Him love on you. You will be surprised at how effective this will be to change your environment, and maybe you too will jump up, shouting that you have just been healed.

Chapter Eight

Outmaneuvering the Manure

THE following story is from my first book in the chapter titled, "Dung":

When I was a pastor in Kansas, I attended a conference in Oklahoma City with a friend of mine from our church. We were also able to view the place where the Oklahoma City bombing had occurred just a few weeks prior.

On our way home, we were driving west on Interstate Forty. There was a southerly wind blowing that day, and the temperature was probably in the mid-seventies. I was driving, my friend was in the passenger seat, and we both had the car windows down. (Since I enjoy fresh air, I would much prefer an open window when the weather is conducive.)

About halfway home, I heard the Lord tell me to put my window up; so after briefly looking around for any potential danger, I then rolled up my window. My friend asked me why I had done this, and I told him that I had an impression from God to do so. He then asked if God wanted him to roll his window up. I responded, "No, just mine."

So we continued on for a bit. I could see in my rearview mirror that a semi truck was rapidly approaching from behind us and was moving over to pass us. As the truck came more fully into view, I could see that it was a cattle truck, which was a common sight in our part of Kansas and this part of Oklahoma.

When the truck passed me, one of the cows had what I can only describe as a *discharge*. That discharge connected with the southerly breeze that was blowing that day and landed squarely on my closed window. It was the worst green, slimy substance that I had ever seen so close up! It was dripping and oozing down my window, and in seconds it completely covered my entire window so that I could not see out of it at all. We pulled over to the side of the road, and I could not even open my door because of the amount of slime.

I can only imagine what would have happened at sixty-five miles per hour if that green substance had hit me in the face. This story would most likely have been told in an obituary! But God was gracious and warned me about it in advance. We had to pull off at the next town and go to a self-serve car wash, where my friend used the carwash to get the car clean so that we could roll down the window and drive in comfort.

Since writing that chapter and publishing that book I have written a study that I will share with you now, one that I am renaming "Outmaneuvering the Manure."

I was in a local church last summer and heard the words to a chorus that went like this: "Father, will you come, and open up our eyes? Fill us with your heart. Renew us with your life."[10] In reality, I am not an expert on all of this, but like you, I am a life-long learner. It's good to learn. The word *learned* means to possess or manifest unusually wide and deep knowledge. There is that word *manifest* that I discussed in an earlier chapter. Deep knowledge sounds kind of philosophical until you realize that the Bible speaks in Psalm 42:7 of the deep crying out or calling out to the deep. For me personally, the deeper I go with God, the more depth I find in Him that is untouched and in some cases undiscovered. The treasure is there, but I must dig deeper to find it.

So I pray and ask God for revelation and more understanding of the deep things of God. I believe that God will answer that prayer and many other prayers because I believe He still speaks today. John 10:27 says that His sheep know His voice, they listen to Him, and they follow Him. Jesus said that His sheep know His voice. I am in that category, and you probably are too. So if you can't hear His voice, maybe you are listening to the wrong voice. Maybe your ears are stuffed and stopped-up, spiritually speaking.

Sometimes ears get stopped up due to strange debris that does not belong in ears.

Read the words of John 10:4–5: "And when he brings out his own sheep, he goes before them; and the sheep follow him, for they know his voice. Yet they will by no means follow a stranger, but will flee from him, for they do not know the voice of strangers."

Now look how verse five reads in The Message Bible: "They won't follow a stranger's voice but will scatter because they aren't used to the sound of it." When my friends call me on the phone, I often recognize who they are by their voice. We don't have caller ID, so voice recognition is important to me. If my phone rings and I answer it and there is a fairly long pause, I recognize that to be a telemarketer and I often hang up before they come on the line. Sometimes I do stay on the line though because I enjoy witnessing to those folks. They are accustomed to having others hang up on them, but they can't hang up on me. I have prayed with many people on those kinds of calls as the Holy Spirit would open up the door, but that is another story for another time.

Another reason we have trouble hearing God is due to what is shared in Isaiah 1:13–17, again in the Message Bible:

> Quit your worship charades.
> I can't stand your trivial religious games:
> Monthly conferences, weekly Sabbaths, special meetings—
> Meetings, meetings, meetings—I can't stand one more!
> Meetings for this, meetings for that. I hate them!
> You've worn me out!
> I'm sick of your religion, religion, religion,
> while you go right on sinning.
> When you put on your next prayer-performance,
> I'll be looking the other way.
> No matter how long or loud or often you pray,
> I'll not be listening.
> And do you know why? Because you've been tearing people to pieces,
> And your hands are bloody.
> Go home and wash up.
> Clean up your act.
> Sweep your lives clean of your evildoings

So I don't have to look at them any longer.
Say no to wrong.
Learn to do good.
Work for justice.
Help the down-and-out.
Stand up for the homeless.
Go to bat for the defenseless.

God is not happy that believers go from one meeting to another, with itching ears, to hear another message and shout amen, but continue living in sin, not changing. It's like spiritual wax building up in our ears. Psalm 58:1–5 declares this, according to the Message Bible:

Is this any way to run a country?
Is there an honest politician in the house?
Behind the scenes you brew cauldrons of evil,
Behind closed doors you make deals with demons.
The wicked crawl from the wrong side of the cradle;
Their first words out of the womb are lies.
Poison, lethal rattlesnake poison,
Drips from their forked tongues—
Deaf to threats, deaf to charm,
Decades of wax built up in their ears.

Jeremiah 6:10 (MSG) adds these thoughts: "It's hopeless. Their ears are stuffed with wax—deaf as a post, blind as a bat. It's hopeless, they are tuned out to God."

Back in 2012 not only did it sound hopeless, but the lack of hearing was so bad that God was actually booed in a national convention. On airplanes, many people now wear noise blockers to drown out the constant roar of the jet engines, and I believe many believers are doing the same when it comes to hearing from God. Some say the Bible is old school. Well, they are half right, but there is a new school in the second half of the Bible too.

There is a funny story that John Wimber told about when he first was converted to Christ. It happened in Las Vegas, and he was at a bar and asked the bartender where to get a Bible. The bartender directed him to a store where he could get one, and when he went in, the clerk helped him find one that said, "Holy Bible: New Testament." John inquired as to what that meant, and the clerk said it was a Bible, or at least half a Bible. John kind of chuckled and asked, what is half a Bible? The clerk did not know, but assured him it was the real thing. Then John asked if it was half price, but the clerk said no. There is a lot more to the story, but to hear it is funny, for sure.

Those who are saved in Jesus should have open ears to hear what He is saying; in fact, John 10:9 declares that they can go in and out and find pasture. Say the phrase "In and out." Say it again three times fast: "In and out. In and out. In and out." Sounds like a cool hamburger joint in California. But the reality is that wherever you are with God, you can find pasture; and wherever there is pasture, the Shepherd is there too, and you can hear His voice. But there is a warning. Watch your step for the cow pies or sheep pies. There is no dung on the door, no slime and no manure stuck to it, as the Door is Jesus Himself.

If you viewed the movie *Back to the Future*, there was a dung-dumping, manure-spreading scene in each of the three movies that kind of made you glad when it always happened to the bad guy or villain in the movie. But do you ever feel that way? Do you feel like life is hitting you after it hits the fan, sometimes right in the face, just like in the previously mentioned movie? Say this right now out loud, with your outside voice: ***"I should move away from the fan. I need to move away from strange voices."*** Look at how Malachi 2:1–3 so vividly puts it:

> "And now, O priests, this commandment is for you.
> If you will not hear,
> And if you will not take it to heart,
> To give glory to My name,"
> Says the LORD of hosts,
> "I will send a curse upon you,
> And I will curse your blessings.
> Yes, I have cursed them already,
> Because you do not take it to heart.
> Behold, I will rebuke your descendants
> And spread refuse on your faces,
> The refuse of your solemn feasts;
> And one will take you away with it."

Spreading refuse on your faces is a picture in *Back to the Future* that I don't want to happen to me. But sometimes it feels like a cattle truck just drove by and my windows were open all the way, and a breeze caught something in the truck, and it wasn't a Holy Spirit breeze either. As I wrote in chapter seven, it was not refreshing in any way.

Just the odor alone would be enough to get me to move far away. First Kings 4:26 says that King Solomon had 40,000 stalls for his animals and horses. Can you imagine cleaning 40,000 stalls each day? Can you also imagine what would happen if those stalls were for some reason not cleaned for just a few days? The stench from that many unclean stalls would be horrible.

There is a waste treatment plant in Omaha, and it sits near a road on which I frequently drive. If the wind is right, you definitely immediately remember that the treatment plant is there. Years ago, while growing up in California in our rural home, we had a septic tank, and one time it kind of got clogged, and we knew it because of the foul odor seeping up from the ground. My dad dug a hole wide enough to get to it with a long stick, but he could not quite reach the clog, so he held me by my legs and lowered me into the hole while I was holding a broom to unclog that mess. I have been gagging every since.

In fact, when our son Jason was a baby and I had to change his diaper, I would always gag in the process. I shared this with our good friend Dr. Bradley, who was our dentist in Houston, and he gave me several masks to wear when changing diapers. So the next time I had to perform that unpleasant task, I put on my mask, and then instead of gagging, I threw up in the mask. Yuck! That was a mess.

When we aren't spending quality time with God and then listen to strange voices instead and fill our lives with worthless stuff, those are the times that our ears get clogged, and life may hit the fan, throwing debris all over us. Had we been immersed in the presence of the Lord, He often would warn us and tell us to put up the window or at the very least show us how to get through the mire without too much of it sticking on us.

Without God, and going through life without a relationship with Jesus (and I will only say this term once for emphasis), it's often like a load of crap hits us squarely in the face. But God can show us how to maneuver away from the manure. From our perspective, when our belongings and our plans, our church, our car, our Facebook page, our iPods and iPads, Kindles, game stations, and Wii, and anything valuable hits the fan, it messes everything up that we call important.

However, in Philippians 3:7–8, Paul says the opposite: "But what things were gain to me, these I have counted loss for Christ. Yet indeed I also count all things loss for the excellence of the knowledge of Christ Jesus my Lord, for whom I have suffered the loss of all things, and count them as rubbish, that I may gain Christ." The King James Version uses the word *dung* for rubbish.

Paul says by inspiration of the Holy Spirit that the things that we call important are not important at all. In fact, they are really rubbish, dung, or manure compared to the sweetness of the Lord's voice and knowing Jesus. What really should be important is our relationship with God, and being able to hear His voice, which should not sound strange to us in any way, because we have had a history of listening to Him for a very long time.

Paul adds in 1 Corinthians 7:35 that we should serve the Lord without distraction. Too many strange voices open the door, or the window, for an unsuspecting wind to blow and dump manure all over you. Let me tell you, that could definitely ruin your day.

John 10:10 assures us that the abundant life comes from talking with Jesus without distraction. He won't dump manure on you, but He will give you hope, love, faith, joy, and contentment, and perhaps even a shovel to help others who do have a load of manure all over them.

Concluding

Let's read Joshua 3:1–5:

Then Joshua rose early in the morning; and they set out from Acacia Grove and came to the Jordan, he and all the children of Israel, and lodged there before they crossed over. So it was, after three days that the officers went through the camp; and they commanded the people, saying, "When you see the ark of the covenant of the LORD your God, and the priests, the Levites, bearing it, then you shall set out from your place and go after it. Yet there shall be a space between you and it, about two thousand cubits by measure. Do not come near it, that you may know the way by which you must go, for you have not passed this way before." And Joshua said to the people, "Sanctify yourselves, for tomorrow the Lord will do wonders among you."

In verse one, the two-word phrase "Acacia Grove" is translated in the King James Version and also the New International Version using the word *Shittim* which is actually a Hebrew word meaning "flesh." You might be able to pick up on a cultural slang word from the first four letters of Shittim, so the meaning "flesh" actually helps you understand how the etymology of words happens. Anyway, the people were moving from Shittim to the Jordan. The Jordan is a picture of the Holy Spirit. The Jordan River is a place where many New Testament baptisms took place, including that of Jesus. We are told in Scriptures that the Jordan River overflows its banks at the time of harvest, so the Jordan literally is a word picture of the Spirit of God. Perhaps God is saying that we need to move from and away from the flesh and into the "Spirit realm." I am confident you see the connection between the words *Shittim* and *dung* and *manure*.

Then they lodged there three days. Those three days are critical in relation to the death, burial, and resurrection of Jesus after three days. The symbolism continues, as we get out of the flesh and into the Spirit, now accessing the power of the resurrection. The passage continues with an emphasis on going after the ark, which is where the presence of the Lord is. Basically, when you see the presence of God, don't waste your time on other things. Move away from the fan, get out of the flesh, and get into the Spirit, moving with resurrection power toward the presence of the Lord. In previous chapters I wrote about the importance and blessings contained within the presence of the Lord.

This passage in Joshua concludes with the thought of sanctification, which really is a fancy word for setting yourself apart unto God. The Word says that if this is accomplished, the Lord promises signs and wonders for you, which often are accompanied by manifestations, all bringing you and others more fully into the kingdom of God, where you can easily and more efficiently outmaneuver the manure. And guess what? It happens through a process called *yielding*.

I have often wondered what would have happened if God had not told me to roll up my window. If I had not listened, and obeyed, what would have happened at 65 miles per hour on Interstate Forty when all that green slime would have hit me squarely in the face? Fortunately, I have learned to hear the Lord's voice, and you can too. You story may not be as demonstrative or as expansive, but I believe it will be timely and save you from horrible consequences.

Move away from the fan.

Close the windows that distract you from Jesus.

Open the doors to Jesus, and go in and out and find good pasture.

Journey

As you evaluate your life right now, I suspect there are some distractions that, if not dealt with, will cause a load of something to hit the fan, and at some point there may be a mess. Why not begin to address that area today, and work toward a lifestyle change that can prohibit that from ever happening? Perhaps it is a bad habit or a mannerism that has been hanging around you for a long time. Maybe it is related to some folks that you have been with, and you know it is time to move away, because the Word clearly says in 1 Corinthians 15 that evil company corrupts good habits. Perhaps you spend too much time with graphic horror movies, or Internet games, or a hobby that takes you away from your family way too often. It could be anything that is trying to separate you from Jesus and kingdom thoughts that produce kingdom life.

I want to help you avoid "dung" times in your life. Remember King Solomon's 40,000 stalls? Well, any of these distractions can cause you to "stall out," spiritually speaking. And then even a mask won't help you much. It's time to clear out the debris and clean out the clutter. Make some room in that stall (or should we call it a manger for Jesus?). Yeah, I know it isn't Christmas now, but the comparison is a good one.

Ask your mate or a good friend to be an accountability partner in this area, and pray together and ask God for His help. If you could get free from it on your own, you would already be free. You need God's help. He is available 24/7. Go for Him now. The goal is to move away from the flesh and more and more into the Spirit.

If nothing else, just pray this simple prayer: Jesus, please help me move away from the fan. Amen.

Chapter Nine

Perversion to Pastor

As you embark on this chapter, please keep in mind some of the thoughts of the previous chapter, as I believe you will see many biblical similarities actually displayed and revealed in the following narrative. This story is written by a personal friend of mine from the upper Midwest region of the United States. Her story is graphic and detailed, yet distilled and reduced in size to accommodate this particular chapter. There truly is substantially more that could have been written and chronicled, but some of the story simply would be too mentally photographic for this setting.

She has asked to remain anonymous, which I have honored; but I want everyone to know I have seen this young lady in action many times, and her faith, determination, and sheer guts for the kingdom are real and genuine. I would not consider sharing her story if I felt even for a moment that there was anything phony about her. She is the real deal and a wonderful example of what Jesus can do with and through a person who will simply yield her life to Him.

Now, here is her account:

> I was five years old when my parents divorced in the mid-'70s. At that time divorce wasn't rampant as it is today. I didn't know any other children whose parents were divorced. This was significant in that the shame, embarrassment, and isolation of the situation helped to breed abandonment, rejection, fear, and confusion, which would completely run my life for many years to come. The truth is that there are large blocks of time in my young life that I don't remember, and the majority of the memories I do recall only serve as reminders of the worthlessness I felt. My parents both remarried and I was lost in the shuffle. I believe there was a demonic assignment on my life.

From a young age, I was marked for destruction through addiction and perversion, but my heavenly Father had another plan. It was around the age of ten that I was repeatedly exposed to pornography outside at the neighbors' while being harassed daily by boys at school. I was very naïve and didn't exhibit any behaviors at that time that would warrant this lifestyle, yet I was absolutely sought out for it.

By the time I entered seventh grade, the harassment became physical and I was groped daily in the halls. One day I remember being surrounded by a group of boys under a staircase. A boy saw what was happening and tried to intervene but was left with a punch to the face (as I remember it) that left him on the ground. That same year I was in art class when a boy who had failed multiple grades physically assaulted me. When one teacher tried to intervene, he threatened her. Sometimes boys would surround me in my classrooms and describe in graphic detail what they were going to do me. The other teachers didn't care and they did nothing.

I was afraid to tell the principal because I was told they would kill me if I did. One day I gathered up the courage to tell my mother. She didn't do anything about it. The harassment and intimidation continued even on the school bus. There too, I was surrounded by boys who would physically hedge me in from every side. It was terrifying. These types of situations only increased in frequency as the years went on and the darkness intensified exponentially.

We moved after seventh grade to Texas. The demonic assignment moved with us, and it wasn't long before it started all over again. The major lesson I was learning was that I wasn't worth protecting. I didn't have value and was totally ignored.

At fifteen I fell in love with a young man my age at school. I knew love for the first time. He invited me to believe that I was special, beautiful, and most important, worthy of love and protection. That love is what sustained me. I was ready to marry him. I gave away my virginity—anything for love. That relationship was everything to me. I began sneaking out of the house multiple times a week to be with him.

It was at that season that I began smoking and drinking regularly. Many mornings I would get to school early under the guise of homework or something else, only to sneak over to his house, which was only a couple of blocks from the school, to do shots of Everclear, an extremely hard alcohol.

On one Friday night that would change my life forever, I snuck out again to meet him. He was waiting outside on his Honda Elite scooter. We headed back to his house, which was only a couple of miles away. I remember passing a gas station on our right where I saw a Camero that for some reason grabbed my attention. A sick feeling washed over me. Moments later we had come up to a stop sign and were preparing to make a left-hand turn into his neighborhood when I heard a car coming fast behind us. I turned around and saw the headlights. I knew that we would be hit. I immediately leaned forward, tightening my hold around my boyfriend and said, "I love you," for the last time.

The next things I heard were screeching tires and shattering glass. Then the lights went out. The next thing I remembered was waking up feeling completely disoriented and confused. I slowly sat up and looked down to see blood everywhere. My left leg above the ankle was in a very unnatural position and was obviously broken. The ambulance arrived, and we were taken separately to an army hospital. I remember waking up in the ER while they were cutting my clothes off and pulling glass and rocks out of my back. The numbness that had accompanied the shock which had protected me from reality was slowly leaving as I was greeted by acute pain.

According to the police reports, I had been thrown the distance of many yards before hitting the ground; they never did recover my shoes. My boyfriend had been thrown backwards into the windshield of the Camero and then bounced into a drainage ditch. Later it was learned the driver was drunk and high. The accident was so devastating that the cops on scene couldn't understand how I survived. And worst of all, my boyfriend, who was only fifteen, died from brain injuries that same night. I was in intensive care when I found out he was dead.

Someone told me they could hear my screams from the waiting room. This was the beginning of an even darker time in my life. My physical recovery from multiple breaks and traumas was prolonged to such an extent that they threatened me with amputation if my left leg didn't begin to heal. Praise God; I have both legs today. However, my emotional healing would take years.

As a young girl I saw dark things in the spirit realm and had strange experiences, and these practices began to increase just before the accident. There was a satanist at my high school who decided he liked me. He was a coke-head and in tremendous bondage. Not long before the car accident, he had invited me to a virgin sacrifice. When I refused him, he threatened me and my boyfriend. I have often wondered about a connection. After the accident, thoughts of suicide would accompany me for years.

My mother, who had been distant, began to try and connect, but it was too late. Something in me died when my boyfriend died. I didn't care anymore. The only love that I recognized was gone. I remember desiring that I was pregnant so I could have someone of my own to love and love me in return—some part of him that I could carry with me.

In autumn, after the accident, I was raped for the first time. I wanted to die. My parents moved us back to Mississippi. I protested; nevertheless, we went back. I was changed. I had left Mississippi terrorized but still longing and desperately wanting the attention of my family. The demonic assignment was still prevailing.

I returned to Mississippi hardened, distant, hopeless, depressed, and angry. The same behavior that previously haunted me in school now seemingly picked up right where it had left off. The harassment returned immediately. It was at this stage that I began to learn about control. Many young men in school tried to dominate me.

For a lot of these young men, the military was the only way out of their poverty, and they had their head start in the ROTC. Because my stepfather was a higher-up in the Air Force, I threatened their future careers, and that seemed to hold many of them at bay. I learned how to protect myself outwardly and to get the attention that I wanted. I also had a new boyfriend. From that time on, I would go from one destructive relationship to another.

At age sixteen I left home to live with my single father in Colorado. He was a minister, though he didn't believe in the divinity of Jesus. I grew up in the church. I had a special love for God as a young girl and my mother would faithfully take my younger sister and me to church. However, despite my church experience, I was crippled by fear. I used to KNOW the presence of evil in my bedroom and would be paralyzed by fear. On one occasion, I woke up floating in the living room. Many years later, I found out the same thing had happened to my sister. The assignment against us was growing in intensity.

As the years rolled on, my world became darker and darker. My addiction to alcohol, pornography, and sex grew and intensified, as did my depression. I went to a lot of therapy over the years, which would only help me on a temporary basis. It always helps when someone listens to your pain, appearing to care, but I liken it to gasping for breaths while drowning.

And after years of abuse by men, I turned to women. This particular demon of perversion had been influencing me since I was very young, and in my early twenties, it took over. I was convinced that being lesbian was my answer. My mannerisms began to change. While my physical appearance was feminine, my personality became more "butch." I "came out of the closet" to a few family members and friends, none of whom seemed to share my enthusiasm.

I fell in love with one girl in particular and would have "married" her if she was open. Praise God; she wasn't. It was toward the end of this season of my life that I encountered a woman who nearly scared me straight. I was in a club in downtown Denver after hours, which was completely normal for me.

There were a couple of female strippers that worked at a local strip club who had just gotten off from work and were having drinks. In my sickness, I was fascinated. I wasn't much different than they were; I just didn't get a paycheck. I was staring at one of them in particular, a very pretty girl despite her zombie demeanor—and that was largely due to the drugs she was on. She glanced up and caught my eye. I asked her a stupid question, I believe regarding her work, and I will never forget the look in her eyes because it scared the hell out of me. Well, almost, anyway. She stared back at me hard and, without any expression, propositioned me sexually. Her words were vulgar and lifeless. It sobered me up almost instantly. There was nothing left in her eyes—just darkness, and darkness completely void of love, life, hope, or worth. I replied with a curt, "Uh, no thanks," and made my escape to the bathroom. I wanted to cry and vomit at the same time. Crude was something I was used to, and I was propositioned often, but this was different. I was terrified because reality had sunk in. If I didn't stop the course my life was on, it would be too late. If I didn't die physically—and believe me, it is a miracle I didn't—I would be just like her, the walking dead. Her eyes and words, laced with demonic oppression, were the beginning of a slow awakening and would haunt me for years to come.

My life was so full of emptiness and chaos that I actually began to contemplate God. I was so sick of the consequences of my choices that I made a mental decision that I wouldn't date anyone else until "the right one."

The right one was a guy in my art class at college. I had not been physically attracted to him, but then I had a dream. I woke up from the dream in love with this man. We were together a few months prior to the end of the school year. He had planned to move out of state that summer. He left for New York, and I went south to visit my grandparents.

While visiting my grandparents, we went to the church where my grandfather had been a pastor for twenty-plus years. Finally, I was now being taught by a true believer in Christ. One day, while sitting in the front pew in this large church I had attended as a child under my unbelieving grandfather, this new pastor gave a message most of us have heard. He told us that we have a God-shaped vacuum in our hearts, and that if we try to fill it with anything but God, we only feel empty and void. Tears streamed down my face as I thought of the untold number of people I'd slept with or the countless nights drunk and getting high. I sat there, all too aware of the deep, dark cavern that was my heart. No one needed to tell me I was a sinner; no one was more aware of that fact than I. The message he gave that day was awesome, and I would love to tell you I gave my heart to Jesus and everything changed. However, there was no altar call or direction of any kind. I left church that day, knowing I needed God, but with no clue how to find Him.

I did begin to talk to God, not Jesus, just God. I told Him if this man wasn't the one, then to please shut the whole thing down before it could go any further, as I couldn't take the pain. My boyfriend moved back, we got a place together, and for awhile things seemed good.

One day, we were driving down the street, and even though everything had been fine, something was now wrong. All of a sudden I had a strong desire to die. I couldn't understand why, as I finally had love and thought that would solve everything. Depression began to rear its ugly head again. The demonic assignment continued.

We were later married in the winter of 1996. Three months later, we were visiting my parents in Minnesota who had moved there from Mississippi not long prior. I was back in my mother's bedroom, and she told me she had been healed of scoliosis. She showed me her spine, and her healing was obvious. That intrigued me, as this was a display of power I had not seen nor heard much about. Up until that point, my opinion and experience of Christianity was that of angry, bigoted, judgmental hypocrites who served an angry, judgmental, powerless god.

Everything was about to change.

I still had physical issues from the accident I had been in, and I asked my mom if her friends could pray for me. She suggested that I go with her to her prayer group the next day. Though very hesitant, I agreed. The next day she took me to lunch before going to prayer. I told her that my sister had informed me that they spoke in tongues at the prayer meeting, and I didn't want any of that.

I distinctly recall the war I literally could feel being waged within me. Part of me wanted to run away, but there was the other part that so strongly compelled me to go, even though I was very nervous. When my mother and I got to the door where the prayer meeting was being held, two women answered, smiling.

The bit that really struck me was they seemed to glow, and love was radiating from them. This was a new experience for me as I had become an extremely hardened individual. They welcomed me in and ushered me into the living room. Ironically, the lady whose home we were in would become my pastor four years later. The other lady was a kind grandmotherly figure who seated herself next to me on the couch. I don't remember much other than her smiling at me and asking me if I had a personal relationship with Jesus. I didn't know what she was talking about. I only knew that I didn't have one.

I had grown up in the church. My father, grandfather, great-grandfather, and uncle were pastors, but I didn't know what she was talking about. Amazingly, that didn't seem to make a difference. Everything in me compelled me to say, "Yes." So I did. And as I responded, I could literally feel a heavy weight lifting off me. No one had to tell me that Jesus was in the room; I knew it. I had an experience of the greatest love I had ever known.

I remember thinking, "I don't deserve this, but someone else does." Even if that wasn't doctrinally correct, I knew that somehow I had just received the most wonderful gift ever and was so grateful. On the drive back to my mother's house, I described my feeling as absolutely euphoric. I told her it was the best "high" I had ever experienced. Later that night, I was so excited to share my experience with my husband. I had tremendous joy and needed to talk to him about it. We later flew back to Colorado with plans to move to Minnesota that summer.

I was still getting drunk in the bars, but now I was telling people about Jesus. It didn't occur to me that the two didn't go together. As I pursued Jesus, my husband pursued Buddha. After we moved to Minnesota, I began to grow in my walk with the Lord, and in a few short years I was delivered from alcohol, cigarettes, pornography, lesbianism, and every other perversion. It was an awesome, amazing experience that only Jesus could provide, and the demonic assignment was now finally broken.

Two years after meeting Jesus and getting saved, I was in a coffeehouse when the Lord told me to go to the restroom and pray. My husband was about to sit at the table of a demonized witch-woman for a reading of some kind. I went into restroom, put my hands up, and began praying, when suddenly I was baptized in the Holy Spirit and received my prayer language. Over the years, I came into a revelation of the Father's awesome love for me and His incredible grace. I'm no longer abandoned, I'm no longer rejected, and I'm no longer fearful or full of shame. I am healed and whole, having forgiven others just as I was forgiven too.

Today, I am married to an awesome, godly man, have a wonderful family, and pastor a church and work with youth and leaders in my community. Father's blessings in my life have been paramount, and though I don't enjoy digging up the past, He showed me that the dung of my past has all served as fertilizer for my future. (Please see Romans 8:28.) I love Father, Jesus, and Holy Spirit more than anything.

Wow, that was some story. Honestly, even though I know her, I don't know whether to cry over all of her circumstances and pain she experienced or rejoice for the new freedom she has found. Along with her story, there are thousands of stories just like hers out there in society today, all with a deep heartache for God. Maybe you have a similar story too that needs to be shared, or perhaps still needs some healing.

The Bible declares in 2 Corinthians 6:1–2, "We then, as workers together with Him also plead with you not to receive the grace of God in vain. For He says: 'In an acceptable time I have heard you, and in the day of salvation I have helped you.' Behold, now is the accepted time; behold, now is the day of salvation."

I really liked her disclosure above: "Over the years, I came into a revelation of the Father's awesome love for me and His incredible grace. I'm no longer abandoned, I'm no longer rejected, and I'm no longer fearful or full of shame. I am healed and whole, having forgiven others just as I was forgiven too."

Colossians 1:21–23 in the Message Bible displays God's covenant like this:

You yourselves are a case study of what he does. At one time you all had your backs turned to God, thinking rebellious thoughts of him, giving him trouble every chance you got. But now, by giving himself completely at the Cross, actually dying for you, Christ brought you over to God's side and put your lives together, whole and holy in his presence. You don't walk away from a gift like that! You stay grounded and steady in that bond of trust, constantly tuned in to the Message, careful not to be distracted or diverted. There is no other Message—just this one. Every creature under heaven gets this same Message. I, Paul, am a messenger of this Message.

Journey

My friend was on a very long journey that no one wants to be on, yet many are, but the message is clear. God can turn that journey around and make something productive, life-receiving and life-giving out of something that otherwise looks worse than a pile of manure coming out of the back of a truck in the movie *Back to the Future*.

How did she get out of that mess? How did she escape the perversion, the drugs, the illicit sex, the binges, and the assignment of the enemy? She had to come to a place where she simply yielded her life to God, and He brought back to her a wonderful yield that demonstrated His love for her, even while she was a sinner. I started this chapter using the phrase "as you embark on this chapter," but let me add here that there may be something in your life that you need to disembark from, get away from, move away from, and distance yourself from. My friend did that. She let go of the past and embraced Jesus.

Romans 5:8 declares, "But God demonstrates His own love toward us, in that while we were still sinners, Christ died for us." Acts 3:19 adds this to the equation: "Repent therefore and be converted, that your sins may be blotted out, so that times of refreshing may come from the presence of the Lord."

This is your day. Your future begins now. Trust God with whatever problem or problems you have carried for so many years. Be honest with Him and just lay it out. I know He will respond. As you disembark from past sins and strongholds and ungodly life-controlling situations, your journey will change with this brand-new step of faith as you simply experience times of refreshing from getting into the presence of the Lord.

You've heard similar messages in previous chapters, but the reality of this truth is that the truth is reality, and I want you to experience this reality with Jesus. God wants it more than you do. He sent His only Son to die for you, but also to be raised up so that you too can be raised up out of your death trap. Eternal life is not just for when you die, but it is for right now. Eternity changes for you as you simply yield to God right now and then sit back and watch how He will work for you.

My pastor, Jim Hart at Eagle's Nest Worship Center in Omaha, frequently states, "If you work the Word, the Word will work for you." I have found this to be consistently true and flawless when approaching anything that life may throw at me.

Take a moment to read Isaiah 55:10–11:

For as the rain comes down, and the snow from heaven,
And do not return there,
But water the earth,
And make it bring forth and bud,
That it may give seed to the sower
And bread to the eater,
So shall My word be that goes forth from My mouth;
It shall not return to Me void,
But it shall accomplish what I please,
And it shall prosper in the thing for which I sent it.

There is a lot of good meat here, but I want you to focus on just one point. God has invested His Word into your life and mine, and He expects a return on that investment. In fact, He proclaims that His Word will not return void, empty, or worthless. I am sure you have heard it said, "What God initiates, He appreciates." And I want to remind you that in addition to being thankful, *appreciate* means to go up in value.

God has planted His word into you right now. You might question how that is possible, but as you have read the previous chapters, then you have also received the Word of God sowed, planted, and now watered in your life, and the harvest is coming. God's harvest, or yield, is always larger than what is planted. It will not return void, and it will accomplish something. And with God it is something BIG! HUGE! GIGANTIC!

In other words, there is a great return on God's investment of His word in your life, and your life is being appreciated even now, going up in value every second you stay engaged with His plans, procedures, strategies, and purposes. It's a win-win situation.

Charles H. Spurgeon declared regarding John Bunyan, "If you cut him, he'd bleed Scripture!" Remember, whatever is in you will come out.

In Luke 8:11, The Parable of the Sower is explained: "Now the parable is this: The seed is the word of God." Remember, if you work the Word, the Word will work for you.

Chapter Ten

Flag Men Ahead

THE worship service at a large Lutheran church in Minnesota was really going strong. The praise band, led by my friend Eric McIntyre, was off-the-chart that evening. There was a level of excitement and anticipation in the air that was contagious. The worship area was really a gym that was set up with chairs in a fan-shaped concourse, with the worship band up on the stage on one side of the gymnasium. The congregation was engaged from the initial note of the first word of the leading chorus. It was definitely an exuberant time of worship, praise, dance, and flags.

After a couple of songs, I stopped the praise band for a moment to share some words of knowledge. These words were very direct, as I either pointed toward people from the front of the church, or in a couple of instances, I walked toward the people and, with the microphone on, shared what I sensed the Lord was saying. One man in particular who was there with his daughter received a word that indicated God wanted him to step out of his comfort zone that evening and jump into all that the Father had for him.

Then we entered into some more fun and upbeat songs, and the crowd continued to be fairly aggressive in their posture and attitude toward worship that evening. I noticed that there were many ladies and children waving flags of all sorts and sizes and shapes. I had observed flags in worship on many prior occasions, but I was about to commence something new, even to me. I once again stopped the worship and gave a very short word of encouragement that flags should not be viewed as something that only ladies and children could participate in, but that men could also be … and before I could finish my sentence, a bunch of men literally jumped out of their seats, charged toward the front, grabbing the remaining flags, and began to run around the worship center like warriors who knew that they were about to encounter the enemy, with full intention of wiping him out.

It was startling, exciting, fun, and crazy all at the same time as so many men directly ran up, seized the flags, and started worshiping with them without any music, singers, or instrumentation. Some were running, while others were jumping. Still others found a stationary place and just waved and beat those flags with such a demonstration. You would have thought that their favorite team had just won a national championship. It was one of the most amazing and exhilarating spectacles I had viewed in a long time.

I love the action of a demonstration in church as people respond to God's presence and shout, praise, and worship in a way that releases power and anointing coupled with faith and expressions of joy. I further enjoy kingdom exhibitions in this realm as they promote the attitude that the enemy is defeated, and that the victory has been won by Jesus Christ, and now it is time to party! The waving of these flags was not just a random act of enthusiasm. It was a specific action of faith that released kingdom life and kingdom miracles into an atmosphere that then set things up for the Holy Spirit to work signs and wonders in the arena where the people were gathering.

The man to whom I had given the earlier word about stepping beyond his comfort zone ended up being the leader of the pack who led a group of men, women, and children running around the building and around those who were seated in the designated chairs for worship. At this point, the band jumped back in, and this ushered in one of the most anointed worship services I had been privileged to be in up to that point in my life, especially during my traveling ministry.

The ministry after the preaching of the Word and the number of healings was awesome that evening. I learned a year later while leading a men's retreat up in St. Cloud, Minnesota, that a certain man's mother was healed of cancer that evening. As I recall, her leg was going to be amputated because of extensive cancer, but God directed me to pray that the cancer would shrink, and that is exactly what happened. It actually shrank back to one inch by one inch in diameter, and then the rest of it was surgically removed microscopically. Another person was healed of asthma, and she returned the next night, testifying that she had not used her inhaler in a 24-hour period and could now breathe freely and easily. The cool thing about that testimony was that we did not pray for healing of asthma, but rather for relief of pain in her back, which also was healed. Isn't God good?

That was simply astounding. Yet, I believe that many things contributed to that healing and others as well, including the boldness of the men that evening who yielded to the Holy Spirit and blazingly opened up the heavens in faith and power by raising up their flags or standards that then chased the enemy from that room and worship area. This allowed more people actually to enter into the presence of the Lord and freely receive from Him in many and various ways.

Most believers have heard or read these words in Isaiah 59:19: "So shall they fear the name of the Lord from the west, and His glory from the rising of the sun; when the enemy comes in like a flood, the Spirit of the Lord will lift up a standard against him." Another helpful reference is Jeremiah 51:12: "Set up the standard on the walls of Babylon; make the guard strong, set up the watchmen, prepare the ambushes. For the Lord has both devised and done what He spoke against the inhabitants of Babylon."

Strong's Exhaustive Concordance of the Bible defines the word *standard* in both of these passages as coming from the Hebrew meaning "flag" or a "flag staff," including a pole with a sail, banner, or flag attached to the pole. These standards or flags were generally used as signals.

The following definitions for the word *standard* come from the *Merriam Webster Dictionary*:

1.
    a: conspicuous object (as a banner) formerly carried at the top of a pole and used to mark a rallying point especially in battle or to serve as an emblem
2.
    a: a long narrow tapering flag that is personal to an individual or corporation and bears heraldic devices
    b: the personal flag of the head of a state or of a member of a royal family
    c: an organization flag carried by a mounted or motorized military unit
    d: banner

3.
- a: something established by authority, custom, or general consent as a model or example: quite slow by today's *standards*

4.
- a: something set up and established by authority as a rule for the measure of quantity, weight, extent, value, or quality

These definitions absolutely epitomize who we are in the kingdom and how we are to respond to various situations, circumstances, and encounters along life's paths. I decided to include all of the definitions to assist us in seeing and carrying the value of such flags in our lives. The kingdom is an advancing army, and our defensive posture, if we have one, is that of rallying others to join us. As with the men in the story above who stormed the altar area to gain access to the flags, which, when unfurled and waved violently, ushered those who were there into the presence of God, so we also carry our individual flags as a sign that we belong to Jesus.

Your flag may come in the form of a testimony or a memorized Bible verse. You may carry it as revelation from a recent sermon or class in which you participated. It could be a song in your heart that when sung always brings you before the King of Kings and the Lord of Lords. Your flag may be displayed in quiet times before the Lord in intercession or simply lying down soaking in the incredible and indescribable recognition of who God is in your life. Then again, your flag may surface every time you dance before the Lord, whether at home in secret or in front of thousands during corporate worship. Whatever the course, and whenever the occasion requires it, your flag is raised as an ensign to declare rank, position, power, and authority.

As I mentioned earlier, Luke 9:1–2 tells us that God has given us power and authority. Power is the ability, might, and strength to complete a task, but authority is the right to use that power. Picture a police officer directing traffic into a Christian concert being held at a local church. The officer has delegated authority given to him, and it is his badge, not his gun, but his badge that backs up that authority. A badge is something worn to show that a person belongs to a certain occupation, school, class, club, society, or organization. In a sense, the badge is a type of flag.

In today's society we often see ribbon types of flags worn on clothing or magnetic ones on cars to symbolize or flag a certain event to the attention of those who see it and recognize it as being authentic for that particular cause. Magnetic ribbons are displayed on cars to endorse certain sports teams or to recognize and welcome those who serve in the military. Pink ribbons draw our attention to breast cancer awareness especially in the month of October.

But let's swing back to the parking lot, where the police officer has gone on a short break. Now there is an eighth grade student directing traffic with a dirty orange flag that was discovered on the side of the road after a previous construction site had been dismantled. This young student with his orange flag has the same authority as the police officer with the badge. It has been delegated to him, and you and I need to honor it as if it were the officer standing there with his badge and his gun. But remember, it is not the gun that enforces the situation, but rather the badge or even a dirty orange flag.

We honor the direction, regardless of the stature. We honor the position, regardless of the person. And we honor God, regardless of how we feel. We raise our flag and wave it high, because the King is in residence there. That phrase came from the Gospel song, "Joy is the Flag."[11] The obvious standard of joy is displayed proudly for all to see. Here are the words:

> Joy is the flag flown high
> From the castle of my heart
> From the castle of my heart
> From the castle of my heart
> Joy is the flag flown high
> From the castle of my heart
> When the King is in residence there
>
> (So) let it fly in the sky
> Let the whole world know
> Let the whole world know
> Let the whole world know
> (So) let it fly in the sky
> Let the whole world know
> That the King is in residence there

I know you want to sing the song, so go ahead and bellow it out. Even if you are alone, let the whole world know that the King is in residence there where you are. Come on, I know you want to. Unless you are like my friend

Teeg, who read my previous book on an airplane with 180 other people around him, I suspect you can at least hum that song, if not be totally lost in the words and melody as you sing your heart out. What's stopping you?

Years ago, when I was on staff at a church in Wisconsin, I learned this little song from a friend named Dave. The song will certainly mess up the spell check on this chapter. It's about a young boy who often would not do his chores, so his mom wrote this little jingle to get him inspired to accomplish those chores. It went like this: "Will ya? Won't-cha? Ain't-cha gonna? If I coax ya, won't-cha wanna? Ah, come on, you said you would! Why don't-cha wanna do the chores you said you would?" The mother always talked about Jesus and encouraged the young lad to give his life to the Lord too.

Later in life, the boy grew up and became a believer in Jesus, but his mom drifted away from God and was now in the hospital, dying due to a terrible disease. So the son went to the hospital to visit his mom, took his guitar with him, and, using the same words that his mom used to say to him, he now sang this song back to her: "Will ya? Won't-cha? Ain't-cha gonna? If I coax ya, won't-cha wanna? Ah, come on, you said you would! Why don't-cha wanna talk about Jesus?"

So, ain't ya gonna sing the song after all of this crazy typing to get these words right? LOL. I will wait for you as you do. You may like it. Raise your hand like a flag and sing it out, for the King is in residence here.

Pause …

Joy is indeed a standard that flags the attention of others, displays who we are as members of the body of Christ, and releases the sweet fruit of the Spirit of joy into the kingdom and into the lives of others that we meet.

Chuck Swindoll, on page 220 of his book, *The Finishing Touch: Becoming God's Masterpiece,*[12] asks:

> How is your sense of humor? Are the times in which we live beginning to be reflected in your attitude, your face, your outlook? Solomon … says three things will occur when we have lost our sense of humor: a broken spirit, a lack of inner healing, and dried-up bones [Proverbs 15:13, 15; 17:22]. What a barren portrait! … Humor is not a sin. It is

a God-given escape hatch ... a safety valve. Being able to see side of life is a rare, vital virtue.

A refreshing sense of humor is never distasteful, ill-timed, or tactless. Instead, it lightens our spirits and energizes our thoughts. It helps us step back and not take this fleeting life quite so seriously.

"Three tests of good humor: Can you laugh at your own mistakes? Can you restrain when it isn't fitting? Can you enjoy it all alone?".... You may feel your strained muscles relax as your troubled thoughts are chased away by good old-fashioned laughter.

Those of you who know me personally or have heard me speak know that I often share humorous stories that have the people laughing and enjoying the message. I heard years ago that if the people will laugh or cry at something you say, they may remember it better. I don't tell jokes or humorous stories to just to make people laugh, as it has to tie in with the message in some way. But I do enjoy flagging certain trigger points in a message that will help drive that point home so that it becomes a reality in the lives of those who listen to it, either in person or later by electronic means.

In 3 John 4, we see what brings the greatest joy to the Lord with these inspired words: "I have no greater joy than to hear that my children walk in truth." Nothing brings a greater celebration of joy to our Father than when He hears that His children (you and I) are walking in truth. Can you see Him raising the joy flag in heaven? Do you see the smile on His face each time that flag is roped up the pole? This is not the same flag that is draped so formally over a casket that is about to be lowered into the ground. This is a flag signaling life. This is a flag that releases favor. This flag of joy is saturated with the Lord's anointing and powers us up with new strength because the joy of the Lord is our strength.

Allow me to conclude this chapter with another flag story, but one that is not as demonstrative, yet just as powerful and with just as much anointing. I was ministering in a Vineyard church in the Boston area, and I shared the story from the beginning of this chapter of my time in Minnesota. At the conclusion of my message, which was about waiting on God, the worship team began to come up to the platform, and I challenged them to remain seated and not to fall into the normal rut where we think we need the music usher us into the presence of the Lord after a message and during prayer ministry. By the way, a rut is nothing more than a shallow grave.

So I just waited in silence, as did the body of believers who were gathered there that day. I would estimate the crowd to be about 250 to 300 people that morning. At one point, a man got up, grabbed a flag, and began to beat the air in a crisscross pattern with that flag. Then another man did the same, followed by more men. Soon we were surrounded by ten to fifteen men beating the air with their flags. The sound of *whoosh, whoosh, whoosh* was all that could be heard throughout the whole worship center. This went on for nearly thirty minutes of constantly beating the air with these flags.

People all around the building began to kneel and pray, some weeping, some praying in the spirit, but all very quiet as the flags continued to be the primary sound that was heard above the intercession that was hitting the room. *Whoosh, whoosh, whoosh,* the sound continued over and over. It was a strong current of wind that was felt concurrently as each man raised and moved his flag with powerful strokes in unison with the others who were doing the same. The presence of God had invaded the room.

After thirty minutes, I invited any in the room who felt they had a call on their lives to preach or teach the word of God to come forward, regardless of whether they had ever taught or preached before in their lifetimes. About thirty people came forward. Then, I invited those who were connected to these folks to gather around them and pray, and many more came forward. The men with the flags now moved forward too and continued to beat the air, but in a much tighter concentric circle around those who felt called to vocally share the Word of God in some fashion. This continued for another twenty minutes or so.

Then, more incredible and amazing ministry happened, with only the beating of the air with the flags as the backdrop, and without any note of music being played, sung, or shared audibly. Yet, I believe all of heaven was singing as the standard of heaven was released and enjoyed on earth in that Vineyard Fellowship in a Boston-area suburb.

Thy kingdom come. Thy will be done on earth as it already is in heaven. Jesus said in John 5:19 that He only did what He saw the Father doing. In Minnesota, the people saw the Father rejoicing and dancing with great music, and it ushered in the presence of the Lord. On the east coast, the people saw the Father moving in almost total silence simply by beating the air with the flags, and it ushered in the presence of the Lord. In each case, as the men yielded to God, that process then brought a tremendous yield from God into each of those settings. The action of using flags was similar, as was the result. But the display of the action was different. Being sensitive to the Holy Spirit and learning to follow His directions will enable you to experience great freedom and joy in your life.

Sometimes in construction zones where there are flagmen controlling the traffic flow, the actual operation of those flagmen is different. Sometimes a handheld sign is used. At other times there is a pilot car or temporary signal light in operation.

As followers of Jesus, we need to caution against going after the methods. We don't follow methods, but we do follow Jesus. Faith is what flags God's attention. Begin to use that flag in your life and you will see amazing, incredible, marvelous, and wonderful things happen as you engage God with your flag of faith.

Journey

Psalm 20:5a out of the Living Translation reads like this: "We will sing for joy when you win. In the name of our God we will lift up our flags." This journey is going to be rather short. It may only be a one- or two-step trip. But those initial steps may indeed launch you on a path, a road, an avenue, and even a transformational highway that could change your life forever.

The yield sign pictured above could be viewed as an emblem or a type of flag. What "yield flag" is God raising in your life right now? Only you can answer that question, but it needs to be answered. Take time to pray and seek the Lord on this. God wants to accomplish the words of Psalm 20:5 in your life and help you raise your flag in victory. But only in yielding to His plan can that victory truly be realized and then celebrated.

> Joy is the flag flown high
> From the castle of my heart
> From the castle of my heart
> From the castle of my heart
> Joy is the flag flown high
> From the castle of my heart
> When the King is in residence there
>
> (So) let it fly in the sky
> Let the whole world know
> Let the whole world know
> Let the whole world know
> (So) let it fly in the sky
> Let the whole world know
> That the King is in residence there

Avenue of Flags (Banners):

My editing consultant Gary Peterson wrote this note in the margin: "Two old hymns I love with references to banners: 'Stand up! Stand up for Jesus' and 'Onward, Christian Soldiers.'" So to honor Gary's suggestion, here is the first verse of each hymn.

Stand up for Jesus
George Duffield and George J. Webb

Stand up, stand up for Jesus,
Ye soldiers of the cross;
Lift high His royal banner,
It must not suffer loss.
From vict'ry unto vict'ry
His army shall He lead,
Till every foe is vanquished,
And Christ is Lord indeed.

Onward, Christian Soldiers
Sabine Baring-Gould and Arthur S. Sullivan

Onward, Christian soldiers, marching as to war,
With the cross of Jesus going on before.
Christ, the royal Master, leads against the foe;
Forward into battle see His banners go!

Refrain:
Onward, Christian soldiers, marching as to war,
With the cross of Jesus going on before.

Chapter Eleven

Study Time: Part 4

WHEN I teach my series of messages called "Willing to Yield," I usually launch with the following story. But when writing this book, I felt I should wait until later to share it. Now it seems appropriate, especially after chapters eight, nine, and ten, and the stories contained in those chapters. Here is the story:

> Three men were riding in their old pickup truck out in the country on some dirt roads when the truck broke down. They searched under the hood to discover the problem. Upon realizing that they needed some parts that they didn't have, they sought to discover how to secure those parts. Trying their cell phones was futile, as they were too far out, so they decided to hoof it into town, which was several miles away.
>
> After walking for a couple of miles, they happened upon an old homestead ranch that had a friendly farmer whom they knew, and they remembered that this particular farmer had some old vehicles in the back forty. So they went up and knocked on the door, hoping the farmer would let them search around for what they might need to fix their own truck.
>
> After knocking on the door and sharing their plight with the farmer, he was gracious and kind and offered to let them go in the back and find whatever they needed. But he also gave them the following warning: His old German Shepherd was back there and would likely bark and possibly even attack them. However, if they proceeded like they owned the place, the dog wouldn't bother them. The three men decided that going back to find the parts and possibly deal with the dog was better

than a very long hike into town on a hot and humid day. They recalled an old saying by an evangelist from the past who often used this statement: "The shadow of a dog never bit anyone."

As the men were glancing around at some of the old rusty and banged-up trucks and cars, they came across an archaic round well with cement casing that had a couple of metal posts near it to help steer people away from the possible danger of this apparently deep well. The men wondered how deep the well might be. One guy found a stone that could fit in his hand, and he dropped it into that old well. They could actually hear it descend down but never heard it hit.

Wow, they thought, *This must be a mighty deep well!* When they looked around for something heavier, they found an old disconnected battery in a truck and proceeded to drop the battery down the well. Once again, they could hear the wind whistling as the battery rapidly propelled downward, yet they never heard it hit.

They looked at each other kind of shocked, so they said to one another that they should find something even heavier. They discovered an old engine block just a few feet away, so they pulled and pushed and heaved and were sweating pretty hard when finally they forced it over the edge of that old well …

Just then, that old dog began to bark and charge at them, running full speed with his tail up in the air, his mane standing straight up, and his ferocious teeth showing. They looked at each other and knew that they could not outrun the dog. So, one man said, "Let's just wait until the dog lunges at us, and we will jump out of the way. Maybe that dog will go down the old well."

So, they held their ground, and sure enough, the dog leaped in their direction. As they jumped out of the way, the old dog went right down into that old well. They heard him go but never heard him hit. Only the barking went from harsh and loud to hushed and finally stilled.

At this point the three guys were feeling kind of guilty, so they decided just to go back on the road and walk toward town without letting the

Study Time: Part 4

old farmer know what happened to his dog. But after a short distance, their consciences got the better of them, so they turned around to face the farmer and share what had happened.

They knocked on the door, and the farmer asked if they found their truck parts. They said, "No, we were just minding our own business and looking around, when suddenly your old dog charged at us. We did not know what to do, so we jumped out of the way, and that dog of yours went straight down that old well out there."

The farmer replied that this was impossible. It just could not have happened that way, but the men insisted, retelling the story again, sharing that the dog lunged at them and then dove down that old well. Once again, the farmer defended his dog and went on to say that the reason that could not have possibly happened is because the dog was tied up with a very long leash to an old engine block.

Remind me, and I will come back to that story with a proper conclusion. In chapter four we learned about Michal the daughter of Saul, and I will continue with more about that teaching and study time as we now look at Acts 7:51: "You stiff-necked and uncircumcised in heart and ears! You always resist the Holy Spirit; as your fathers did, so do you."

This verse comes in the middle of a great message or sermon that Stephen was presenting. Now, we aren't told if this was his first message or his hundredth, but it is a good message, for sure. And at this juncture in the message, he was really challenging the religious crowd of that day. He presented an interesting case study for them and perhaps even more so for us. He simply stated that they resisted the Holy Spirit in the same way that their fathers did.

Most people would agree that certain illnesses come or flow through various family lines. Cancer comes through family lines, as do diabetes and heart disease. Now, we learn that resisting the Holy Spirit also comes through family lines. This helps to explain why Michal was referred to as the daughter of Saul. It brings understanding to her situation. It doesn't excuse her, but it does help in our biblical comprehension of the story.

In my family, there are several physical problems that have come through the family lines. One of them was hernias. My dad had two or three, I have had four, and I know other members of the extended family have also had some. But prior to our son being born, we prayed against this generational curse, breaking the power of it; and to date, with Jason going on twenty-two as I write this, he has not had one hernia-related problem. Personally, I had two before I was six years old.

There are several other maladies that have come through my side or my wife's side of the family. So we prayed against those over Jason as well. For instance, Diane and I both wear glasses, but Jason's ongoing eye exams reveal that he has 20/15 vision, which actually is better than 20/20. A person with 20/15 vision can see objects at 20 feet that a person with 20/20 vision can only see at 15 feet. **Now, that is amazing. Come on, God!**

Basically, what Stephen was saying was that these religious leaders were being inflexible, unwilling to change, and certainly unable to move and flow with the Holy Spirit. I guess we could honestly appraise the situation and say that they simply weren't yielding.

Now, let's read verses 54 to the end of the chapter:

> When they heard these things they were cut to the heart, and they gnashed at him with their teeth. But he, being full of the Holy Spirit, gazed into heaven and saw the glory of God, and Jesus standing at the right hand of God, and said, "Look! I see the heavens opened and the Son of Man standing at the right hand of God!"
>
> Then they cried out with a loud voice, stopped their ears, and ran at him with one accord; and they cast him out of the city and stoned him. And the witnesses laid down their clothes at the feet of a young man named Saul. And they stoned Stephen as he was calling on God and saying, "Lord Jesus, receive my spirit." Then he knelt down and cried out with a loud voice, "Lord, do not charge them with this sin." And when he had said this, he fell asleep.

Please allow me to unpack this a bit for you. Stephen had a vision while preaching, and this just aggravated the religious crowd even more. I have a teaching message called "Bypassing Religious Symbols and Hype" that more clearly identifies some of these traits, but it is clear that this crowd is elicit and wants revenge. I am sure you can visualize the crowd seething and hissing and booing and shouting in their outrage.

But in this vision, Stephen sees something that probably to this point has never happened before. Let's superimpose some imagination into the story at this point, or as my pastor likes to say, some attitude.

Pretend you are in heaven, and you have already passed to afterlife with a firm belief of Jesus Christ as your Savior and Lord, having previously repented of your sins and having had a solid relationship with Jesus before your death. Now, you are in heaven, and there is rejoicing, shouting, praying, and worshiping going on 24/7, except there is no concept of time there like we know it on earth.

Suddenly, there is a hush. Everyone is staring and looking to see what is happening, and those who are up there begin to question among themselves and talk with others, asking if anyone knows what is happening. Up to this point, Jesus has always been seated at the right hand of the Father, but now He is standing. It appears that He is looking at someone. Can anyone see who He is looking at? As others draw closer, they respond that it appears He is looking at someone down on earth, but who could it be? We know because we have the narrative of what happened, but for the folks in heaven this was definitely a new experience.

I think that Jesus actually stood up in honor for the first New Testament martyr. I believe this with all of my heart. I can't come up with any other explanation. Can you imagine Jesus Christ, the risen King of Kings and Lord of Lords, Who did everything possible for our salvation and Who concluded simply with the words, "It is finished," now standing in honor of someone else? This is mind-boggling. All I can say is, *Wow, that's cool, amen, amazing, awesome, incredible, fantastic, unreal, powerful, sweet, unbelievable, and implausible.* Okay, you get the picture. *Significant, magnificent, out of sight, crazy, right on, groovy, gnarly dude …* better stop now.

And they started to stone him. Since we are talking about stones and rocks, let me landscape you another scene. Once in a while, as I have been using my power lawnmower, a tiny pebble will shoot out from the blades like a projectile aimed directly at my shins, and it is a direct hit. Wow, does that ever hurt! And this is usually followed by a trickle of blood cascading down my shins.

Years ago, while riding my bike in a summer school bike class at my middle school, I was pedaling through some loose gravel when my chain came off, causing me to crash into that gravel and really tear up my knee. I had a definite gash, and it was bleeding profusely. I actually had to take off my shoes and socks and use the socks to apply direct pressure to slow down the bleeding.

With my bike in a broken state, I had to push it all the way home; and I am not kidding: It was a twelve-mile hike, stopping every few feet to mop up more blood. I have a scar on my knee to this day from that injury.

Can you imagine people charging at Stephen with rocks and stones that they could hold in their hands? What would you be doing? I think I would be running as fast as I could. But Stephen stood there praying. Read those verses again:

> And they stoned Stephen as he was calling on God and saying, "Lord Jesus, receive my spirit." Then he knelt down and cried out with a loud voice, "Lord, do not charge them with this sin." And when he had said this, he fell asleep.

Notice what and how he prayed. He asked God not to charge them with this sin. Either he was crazy or there was simply another reason why he could do this in the face of such audacious and sadistic physical and painful attacks. We will look at that reason soon. But first, let's examine the answer to this simple yet anointed prayer. The answer lies in verse 58: "And they cast him out of the city and stoned him. And the witnesses laid down their clothes at the feet of a young man named Saul." And God answered the prayer. With my previous depiction of heaven, I now see Jesus standing and now turning to the Father, saying, "Let's work on Saul." After all, Saul is a primary inciter of religious strife that is evidenced in ongoing killing and slaughtering of early Christians in that day. Jesus says, "Let's convince Saul and see his life turned around even while Stephen is dying."

The prayer was answered. After Saul had a life-changing Damascus road experience, he became known as Paul. He then wrote a large portion of the New Testament, and he ministered all through the region and established many churches. Because of his anointed travels and writings, he probably enabled more people to come to know Jesus than all the great evangelists who have ever lived.

But now it is time to discover what really motivated Stephen to be able to preach this great message and die this harsh and cruel death, yet relying on and trusting in Jesus at the same time. The answer is in Acts 6:1–4: "Now in those days, when the number of the disciples was multiplying, there arose a complaint against the Hebrews by the Hellenists, because their widows were neglected in the daily distribution. Then the twelve summoned the multitude of the disciples and said, 'It is not desirable that we should leave the word of God and serve tables. Therefore, brethren, seek out from among you seven men of good reputation, full of the Holy Spirit and wisdom, whom we may appoint over this business; but we will give ourselves continually to prayer and to the ministry of the word.'"

As you have just read in the story, the church in the early days was growing by the thousands so rapidly that a lot of ministry to some of these new believers was being neglected. It probably wasn't intentional, but rather there was this new excitement and enthusiasm in town about what was happening with people coming to know Jesus. A decision had to be reached and an answer had to come forth, so the whole group of disciples got together and decided to select seven new leaders with three specific qualifications. They had to be full of the Holy Spirit (not full of themselves, like Michal was), and they needed to have a good reputation, plus the ideal candidate would also have wisdom.

This is the key: wisdom. You may remember that we launched the first study time with James 3:17, which stated that a person of wisdom was first "willing to yield." Stephen was the perfect candidate, as he yielded to the point of death. Remember some of our previous points about "whatever is in you is going to come out." Wisdom was in Stephen, and it came out or manifested in the form of yielding to God. He did not run in the face of adversity, but rather stood his ground. Like the Egyptian slaves who had entered the Promised Land as actual "landowners," here Stephen was also representing the spiritual application to this same premise of being a landowner who was not going to back down. As the Bible says Ephesians 6, having done all to stand, we will stand. That is our position. Unless, of course, you don't have that wisdom. Then you will probably have a problem.

On April 20, 1999, two girls at Columbine High School were faced with a similar situation. The first girl acknowledged Jesus and was immediately shot. The second girl, after just having seen her friend shot to death, was asked the same question as to whether she too believed in Jesus. She also stood her ground, proclaiming that she loved Jesus, and was immediately shot and killed. If there aren't tears in your eyes right now, something is wrong, dear friend. Yet, too often we can't yield to God at church to offer to pray for someone who looks a little discouraged or to stick up for the pastor when he or she is the victim of vicious gossip.

It is time to conclude this study time with two verses out of Galatians 5. The first is in verse 7: "You ran well. Who hindered you from obeying the truth?" Now let's read it from the Message Bible: "You were running superbly! Who cut in on you, deflecting you from the true course of obedience? This detour doesn't come from the One who called you into the race in the first place."

I am sure you know of people who used to run well when it came to their lives with Jesus. They were active in their faith, sharing and witnessing, attending prayer meetings, worshipping the Lord, and extending outward whenever possible. But along the way, something happened. Something strange happened, and they slowly drew back, became spiritually withdrawn, and were seen less and less until one day they stopped showing up at all. Paul writes in Philippians 3 that we all are to run as ones who will finish the race.

Literally, we all need to work at finishing well. Jesus was and is the Author and Finisher of our faith. Remember, God did not rest because He was tired but because He was finished.[13] Jesus said He came to finish the work of the Father. Remember, God did not rest because He was tired, but because He was finished. Bet you thought that was an unedited miss in this book, but it was intentional to drive the point home.

Stephen finished well, as did the girls at Columbine High School, but Michal did not finish well and was barren with no new life until the day of her death. Samson did not finish well, either. Oh, yes, he defeated the Philistines, which was the call on his life from the womb. However, Samson's eyes were gouged out, and he died when the building collapsed on him. It would have been far better had he accomplished the God-given task and lived to tell about it while holding and seeing his grandchildren.

The other verse from Galatians 5 is in verse 1: "Stand fast therefore in the liberty by which Christ has made us free, and do not be entangled again with a yoke of bondage." This is a critical verse and must be examined as we conclude. The best way to stand fast is not to return to something from which you have been delivered (like a dog returning to its vomit). According to Jesus, whom the Son sets free is free indeed (John 8:36). So stay free.

Study Time: Part 4

Remember the dog story at the beginning of this chapter? Whatever you are tied to will take you there. I repeat: Whatever you are tied to will take you there. So get and stay tied and connected to Jesus. John 15 teaches us that Jesus is the Vine, and we are the branches connected to the Vine. Staying connected is the key to learning how to yield.

Journey

This is a tough journey isn't it? Most would agree that our goal is to lay our lives down for Jesus, yet even in the simple things we often fall way short. How can we overcome those obstacles and keep running strong? How can we learn to stand, not giving the enemy an inch of ground, while walking in truth and humility? It really is a tough road to follow, and no common antidote or fancy quote will make it easy for us at this point. It must be a raw and obvious life choice for this to happen. We must trust God. We must trust and obey, as the old hymn stanza melodiously commands. Except, there is no orchestra and no band, only a strong, silent commitment and salute to the flag that is flown over the castle of our hearts. It is a rigorous road that is embedded with potholes and snares of the enemy, with hidden bombs ready to detonate if we veer off course. And yes, even a trap door that will drop us like a rock, perhaps even an old engine block, into a deep cavern.

But if you look up, you may just see Jesus standing on your behalf too. He likes to do those things, and like Moses when his hands were raised and the battle was won, so with Jesus praying on our behalf and interceding to the Father according to Romans 8, our victory is secured, our borders are fortified, our army is ready, and we are winners. That may sound simplistic, but it is the truth. No weapon formed against us will prosper, according to Isaiah 54:17. We are more than conquerors (Rom. 8:37).

Are you ready?

Take time right now to stop and pray the most honest, authentic prayer you have ever spoken, and tell God the truth. He already knows it, but He wants to hear it from you. Tell Him where you are, and ask Him to help you get to where He wants you to be. God gave us a guarantee when He said in 2 Corinthians 1:20, "For all the promises of God in Him are Yes, and in Him Amen, to the glory of God through us."

Notice that He gives the promises and backs them up, but they manifest through us. Just like King David, James, and Stephen as they came to pass through them, so they will also happen through us. Get attached to God in prayer, because whatever you are tied to will take you there. It's time to yield in prayer. Please don't turn that page until you pray—it is too important. There may be someone right now looking at you as a possible candidate to be with a group of people who are chosen because they are filled with the Holy Spirit, have a great reputation, and have a lot of wisdom. To avoid being derailed by the enemy, yielding to God will keep you on track.

CHAPTER TWELVE

TAKING COURAGE

THIS particular chapter takes on a different tone, in that some of it is actually written by friends and acquaintances of mine. I asked these folks to send me testimonies of times when they actually reached out to strangers or to folks they barely knew with the power of the kingdom of God, along with the ensuing results. They have agreed to do so with the understanding that only their first names and locations would appear in the book. I hope you discover insights that are helpful, while simultaneously enabling you to identify with some of these folks as they took steps of faith and courage.

Frequently, I hear people praying for courage, and of course we can pray for anything that pertains to the kingdom along with life and godliness. But the reality is that many people in the Bible were simply courageous in their acts of obedience. In Acts 28:15, Paul stated that he took courage. Joshua was instructed by God to be courageous and strong, and then to be *very* courageous and *very* strong. God did not tell Joshua to *pray* for courage as they disembarked from the wilderness and launched into the Promised Land. He told him to *be* very courageous.

To illustrate this principle, I will share a very lame story. Many years ago, when I was on staff at a church in Houston, the Beekeepers Association wanted to rent our building for monthly meetings. There was a lot of discussion about whether the church wanted to set a precedent and start renting out the facilities to nonreligious organizations. Finally, after much discussion, it was time for a vote. I raised my hand and interjected that I wanted to make sure I understood the vote, which was, as I asked, "To Bee or not to Bee?" My mother-in-law Ruth would say, "That was a *groaner!*"

It was funny at the time, but it does help to drive home the point that

God calls on us to be obedient in our walk with Him. You have already read in previous chapters many examples of this courageous credential. These stories will more fully demonstrate to us that part of our character as believers is to be courageous, walk boldly, and act dauntlessly as a part of the banner over our heart. So, let's join my friends in their journeys that spotlight times of radical obedience by yielding to God at a moment's notice and then fully realizing and obtaining God's return yield back into their lives and the lives of those being touched by the presence of God at that distinct and precious moment.

> Two years ago I attended a healing conference at a church in central New Jersey. I had expected teaching on healing and then an opportunity to pray for healing. But, to my surprise, the speaker, Rev. Jack Sheffield, said we were going on an "Ultimate Treasure Hunt." I was surprised. I had no idea what that was, but I listened to his teaching. He said we should pray as a congregation and ask for words of knowledge.
>
> To me this was an unusual request, but I decided to be a bit adventurous and try it. I believed the Holy Spirit gave me two words of knowledge: The color *yellow* and the words "she came twice." This had no particular meaning to me, but I gave the words of knowledge to a small group.
>
> Then Pastor Jack told us to go out into the neighborhood and find someone who fit this word of knowledge. I went with two strangers to a nearby corner delicatessen. This was a popular place, with people coming in and out. After about ten minutes with not much happening, a young woman came by, went into the deli, bought something, and then left. As she left, I noticed she was wearing yellow.
>
> A few moments later, seemingly out of nowhere, she returned to the deli, and this time she said hello to us. I and the others said hello back and told her we were there on behalf of a local church telling people about Jesus. Suddenly, this woman wept and asked us to tell her more about Jesus, and we led her to faith in Jesus as Savior and Lord. My understanding is that she went back to that church two Sundays later. The word of knowledge came into being, much to my surprise and delight, and the Lord received someone new into His Kingdom.
>
> *- Fred from New Jersey*

As we started making plans to take a trip to Florida, I prayed that it was God's will for us to go. A refund from our utilities company came several days after we decided to embark on this journey. My husband had figured about how much gas we might need to make the trip. The amount of the check was almost exactly the amount Al had calculated. It confirmed to me that was a "God" sign.

As we traveled down south, we called ahead to the town where we might arrive for the first night's lodging. It seemed to me the lady answering the phone was a little rude, but upon Al's request, I was to call her back for further pricing. I had to pray, "Lord, remove my pride and let me have compassion for this lady as You have loved her." This was the hotel where we would later stop for the night. Two ladies, an older and a younger gal, greeted us upon arrival.

In the morning, we went for a very early breakfast to be able to get started on the road. The younger gal was just getting started setting out the items, but she proceeded to talk about herself as she worked. This delay created an opportunity for us to visit with her, discern spiritual needs, and learn facts about which we could pray for her. It was an encounter that I definitely feel was a "God" planned meeting.

-Joyce from Nebraska

I had been in worship one Sunday, and I saw this woman, this cashier, during worship. In my Spirit, I had this vision of this woman whom I didn't really recognize. Perhaps I'd seen her and my memory was being refreshed or something, but I didn't remember knowing her.

Later that week, I was walking into a grocery store, and lo and behold, I saw that very cashier as I walked in the door. I had no idea what I was supposed to say to her or anything, and I was in a big hurry. But I got the couple items I had to get, and made my way to the check stands, pretty sure that since I didn't know what to say, that I should just kind of chalk this one up to my imagination or save it for later and get out of there.

But she had the shortest line by far, so I was destined for her line. It only made sense. I was praying pretty feverishly for something, anything, to say to her as I waited for the one person in front of me to wrap up the purchase, but the only thing that was coming was that I was supposed to reassure her, connect with her, and offer prayer—but I wasn't getting anything specific. So she was checking my groceries, and I didn't have much stuff, but I knew I better have something to say—that this was an assignment, and I didn't want to blow it.

What ensued was the single worst act of evangelistic outreach in the history of Christian kind. I said something like, "Hey, uh, I just, was praying, you know, and, this might seem kind of weird, but I think God gave me a vision of you." Her eyes instantly said, "Oh, man, you are a gigantic creep, aren't you?" I suddenly realized that I might have been sounding like I was giving a terrible pick-up line, so I, through stammers, started pointing at my wedding ring and saying something like, "But, listen, I'm married, and I don't mean this to be weird." She was getting ever more perplexed because this was so disjointed and horrible.

It's worth mentioning at this point that I am not someone who is short of words or composure. I was a communications major in college and spent eight years on the radio. I know how to use my brain and my mouth to make words that make sense. But in this moment, I was a buffoon's buffoon.

So I said something like, "This isn't coming out right, but I am a Christian and I kind of think I am supposed to pray for you." I wrote down my number as she wrapped up my transaction, and I gave it to her. She said "thanks" in the way that someone might say "thanks" if you had just handed her a cardboard box full of horse manure.

So I was praying as I left the store, "Oh, God. Oh, God. Oh, God. Oh, God. Please make that somehow not horrible for her. Please say I didn't just drive a wedge between her and You."

But listen to this.

The next day, my phone rang. And it was her. And she told me her story. She had a long one, full of pain and serious issues: a dad whom she cared for full-time in declining health, husband issues, financial issues, kid issues, all kinds of really acute stuff. She welcomed the prayer, and as bad as my carrying out of my assignment was, it was still an encouragement to her that her prayers were being heard by God—that He was and is real.

~ Teeg from Nebraska

One thought that comes to mind is an opportunity to pray with one of our guests at our camp here. A young man and his wife have been coming every year to our camp, and we have become good friends with them. I went down to their cabin to bring them a couple of mousetraps, as they had seen one of those critters running across the floor. I asked the man if he wanted to set the traps or if he wanted me to do it. His wife said he couldn't really set them because his one hand was in so much pain. I asked what was wrong, and he said he had been helping a friend with some carpentry work before coming on vacation, and while sanding a board, a large, long wood sliver went deep into the palm of his hand. He was in excruciating pain. The doctors hadn't wanted to operate and take it out because they were afraid of damaging muscle and nerves in his hand. They wanted it to push itself out.

His wife asked him if he wanted her to take him home, and he declined, saying he might as well be here at camp rather than at home in agony. I asked to see it, and he laid his hand in my open hand. While I was looking at it, the Lord spoke to my heart to pray for him. I asked him if I could pray for him. They both said, "Yes." I asked the Lord for a supernatural extraction, and I commanded all pain to go in Jesus' name. It was a short prayer, but I felt the agreement of the Spirit. When I opened my eyes, they were both smiling at me. I could tell they were not accustomed to prayer.

A little while later we went with them to our favorite blueberry patch to pick berries. I continued to beseech the Lord on his behalf, thanking God for showing His love to this precious man.

That evening he came into the lodge office and asked for me. He hemmed and hawed around in an embarrassed sort of way, not quite knowing how to express what was in his heart, until finally he said, "Uh,

I uh, I'm not very religious, I mean I don't go to church and all ... but you know that thing you did with my hand?" (I knew he meant the prayer.) I said, "Yes?" He said, "Well, about twenty minutes after you prayed, all the pain left. I have no pain in my hand."

I exclaimed, "See, God LOVES you—He really LOVES you!!" He was all smiles.

The doctor finally took the splinter out surgically because it didn't come out on its own, and each year he brings that splinter with him up to camp in a jar as a little reminder of what God did. He is still amazed. I was so filled with joy that he could experience God's power and love.

~Daryl from Canada

An elderly woman approached me during some ministry time after I had gotten done preaching. Through the translation of her daughter, she told me, "You said that God would heal us if we needed healing." I replied, "Yes, ma'am, God desires for everyone to be made whole."

"Well, I want God to heal me."

"God wants to heal you; what is wrong with you?" I replied.

Her response shocked me for a moment: "I'm blind, and I want to see again."

As I said, I was taken back for a moment because, up to this point in my life, I had never prayed for blind eyes to see, but I knew God's Word. I knew if Jesus did it, then He desired for it to be done again. So with a new faith and courage rising in me, I placed my thumbs on her eyes, "In the name of Jesus, eyes, SEE!" I took a step back and asked her if she could see anything.

After blinking several times, a small smile appeared on her face, and she said, "I am starting to see light."

I put my thumbs on her eyes once more and said, "God is a God of completion." One more time I spoke to her blindness, "In the name of

Jesus, eyes, SEE!" I took two steps back and held up my hand, asking her if she could see anything better.

I watched in total amazement as big tears filled her eyes. She reached out and grabbed my hand, looking directly at it and then at me. She said, "I can see. I CAN SEE!!!" She and her daughter wept and rejoiced and glorified God for the miracle He performed in her life.

~ TW from Nebraska

We were walking through the bush, visiting the houses that we came across, asking people if they would like prayer. We were told there was a woman who lived not too far from where we were and that she was dying. We walked through the bush until we came to a clearing. It was a typical mud hut of the Niassa Province in Northern Mozambique, Africa.

Being invited in, we found a woman who was lying on the dirt floor on a bamboo mat. She had not been able to get up for three months. Her husband was quite worried about her. We asked if we could pray for her, and he reluctantly agreed. He was from a different religion and was not too sure about Christians.

We went into the little dark mud hut where there was a smoky fire going, and we knelt and sat on the dirt around the lady. She couldn't have weighed more than eighty pounds, and her legs were about as big around as a broom handle. We told her Jesus loves her and that we were going to pray and ask Him to heal her. The smoke from the fire filled the room and stung our eyes, but we ignored it as best as we could.

We prayed for a few minutes and then asked her how she felt. She said she might try to sit up. So we helped her sit up. We prayed a bit more, and then she decided she might try to stand, so we helped her stand. We prayed some more and asked how she was. She then wanted to go outside, so we walked with her outside. It was the first time she had been up in three months!

She sat on a mat and Catherine, one of the team members, washed her feet. Her feet were dirty, covered with feces, etc. It was a very touching scene.

We talked to them about Jesus, and the husband said, "Well, you know I am a Muslim, but I believe I like this Jesus." We prayed with them to receive Him as their Savior and then introduced them to the local pastor. We told them to call him when they wanted prayer. He will look in on them and shepherd them, and we left them in his care.

~Jim from Mozambique

One day several months ago, I walked into our bank, and I found myself before a new teller whom I hadn't seen before. She had an accent. I asked her where she was from. "Cuba," she answered. I replied, perhaps a little flippantly, "Atheist, huh?" She said that yes, that is the official government stance, but not all Cubans are atheists.

I then said (and I don't know why I said it—perhaps it was a word of knowledge), "Do you have pain in your body?"

She answered, "Do I ever have pain! It's non-stop. I have kidney disease, and it is incurable."

I said, "Would you like to be healed?"

"Yes," she replied.

Then I reached over the counter, touched her lightly, saying, "Be healed." She looked surprised, then confused, then delighted. "The pain is gone." She exclaimed.

"Jesus just healed you," I explained.

One week later, I was back in the bank. I had forgotten the incident. The same teller was there. She spotted me, saying, "It's you! Do you know what happened? I am completely healed—no more pain, and the doctor says my kidneys are perfect. I told all the employees in the bank, and they are all blown away."

* * *

Now picture this scene: Two elderly ladies at McDonald's doing calisthenics, and deep knee bends, overjoyed at God's goodness. How did this come about? Well, it happened recently when Sue and I dropped in to a local McDonald's for a quick burger. We began chatting with two ladies sitting at an adjoining table. One of them happened to mention that they both suffered from arthritis and fibromyalgia. My ears perked up. "How long have you both had these conditions?" I questioned. They replied that it had been several years for both of them. I asked them if they would like to be completely healed. "Of course," was the reply, in unison, "but that would be impossible."

"With Jesus it is possible," Sue and I said. "Here is our proposal. Would you allow Sue and me to pray a brief blessing on you both? If you do, Jesus will do the rest by healing you completely."

They agreed. We commanded the arthritis and fibromyalgia to go and for the joints and muscle tissue to be restored. Then we asked them to test it out and to begin to exercise. The startled expressions on both their faces were priceless. They were exercising vigorously. Overjoyed and ecstatic, they began thanking Jesus right there in public, free from pain and immobilized joints.

* * *

On another day at the lunch break, we were in a restaurant. The server, who was also the owner of the restaurant, complained of constant pain and swelling due to osteoporosis and osteoarthritis. We offered to pray for her, and God healed her on the spot.

She came back to our table five different times to tell us with astonishment that the swelling was gone, the pain was gone also, and her body was completely functional. She kept asking, "What is the electricity that is still pulsating through my body?" We told her that the healing and the power was Jesus on the outside and then asked her if she would like to have Jesus on the inside. "Oh, yes," she declared, "could I?" She prayed with us, repented, believed, and was born again. She then went over to get her daughter, who was also working in the restaurant, so she could also receive healing. Jesus did the rest.

- Bob and Sue from Canada

One morning my family and I took a walk to a grocery outlet. On the way, we stopped by the Buddhist temple down the street and prayed over a guy working in the garden because his back was hurt. I was not sure if he was healed or not. We got to the grocery parking lot, and we asked a guy if he would like prayer. He mockingly responded, "You can pray for me to get drugs." I shared with him what the Lord was doing, and he changed his attitude a little bit.

Inside the store, we prayed over a guy who tore his meniscus. We prayed over him and all the pain left. He was shocked and said we should come in there every week. On our way back, that guy who asked for drugs was still sitting in his car. We shared with him what happened in the store, and he let me pray over him. He said he felt God's presence.

We came across two girls and asked if we could pray for them. One girl said she was an atheist, so I said, "Cool, let me bless you anyway. You don't have to believe me." I prayed. Then, the Lord revealed to me that she was an artist whose art was like poetry and that she was also the shoulder to cry on for her friends. I started getting more in depth about how God made her, and she was tripping out.

She asked how I knew all this stuff about her. I told her that the God she didn't believe in loves her so much that He's sharing that stuff with me. Then I asked her if she had any pain in her body, and she said her back hurt. I prayed and the Lord healed her back. She said she felt all light. I then saw how she had religion forced on her and that she had a negative view of who God is, so I shared the gospel and told her how she could know Him. I didn't force anything on her but just demonstrated God's goodness in a way that she couldn't deny, leaving her with the choice she has to make.

~Joshua from Oregon

Daily living in the supernatural can start with a couple simple questions: "Can I pray for you?" "Can I pray for you now?"

I saw a guy at a supermarket sniffling and rubbing his nose. I asked if he was ill. "I have a severe cold," he spoke in a groggy voice.

I told him that Jesus could heal him right now and asked, "Can I pray for you?"

He said, "Yes."

I asked, "Can I pray for you now?"

Again, he said, "Yes."

I prayed for him, and his sniffling nose immediately cleared up. The constriction on his voice was gone, his headache was removed, and he breathed freely.

Just a couple of simple questions can lead to a changed life forever. I found out he was saved, and we rejoiced together.

-Jeff from California

Recently, I was at a hotel in Salina, Kansas, which was directly across the street from the Greyhound bus depot area for Salina. As I walked to my car to get one more item for the hotel room, I was drawn to a man standing in the entranceway of the hotel. So I struck up a conversation with him and discovered that he was a Greyhound bus driver and that he would often use this hotel to sleep and rest in before his next run. Over the course of our discussion, I learned that he was tired of his job and needed some financial relief and more time with his family. I then offered to pray with him for these needs, and he readily accepted. When I concluded the prayer, he grabbed my hand and shook it vigorously, thanking me repeatedly for the prayer, practically shouting and declaring that I had no idea how much he needed that prayer.

Later in the evening, I met a man in the spa and pool area and struck up a conversation with him. He was a representative for Braum's Ice Cream, which happened to have a franchise store right next to the hotel. As our conversation continued, I offered to pray for his success with that company. Later in the evening, I bumped into him in the hallway, and he asked me to pray for his daughter at home in Arkansas who had gone into premature labor. After our prayer, we said goodnight, but he added that he would like to join us for breakfast in the morning.

The next morning he came and sat at our table and shared that his daughter was doing great and did not deliver the baby. I then offered him a copy of my recent book *Downloads from Heaven*, and he promised to read it. About three months later, I received an email from him thanking me for the book and sharing how much various chapters had meant to him.

* * *

Once on a trip to Victoria, Texas, I was engaged in conversation with the manager at the hotel where I was staying, and I learned that she and her husband were trying to have a baby. I offered to pray with her for that, and a few months later I received an email confirming her pregnancy with a note thanking me for the prayer.

* * *

One time on an airplane, I was witnessing to the person sitting next to me, and at one point I decided to ask that person if he might like to pray to get tight with God and to get right with Him too. Just as I was about to start the prayer, someone in the seat behind me reached up and tapped me on the shoulder, and as I strained to look back to see what this person wanted, it was a man who simply asked, "Can I be included in that prayer too?" The point is that we often aren't aware of who else may be watching, and God can use your courage and your faithfulness to attract the Holy Spirit to someone else that you aren't even specifically sharing with at the time. He is so amazing. I am sure you agree.
 -*Jay from Nebraska (Wait—that's me, the author of this book! LOL!)*

About a year ago, Jason and I decided we wanted to lead a healing service on Facebook. We selected an evening to host it and began to let our friends know, encouraging them to share it with their friends too. We listened in advance to some praise and worship music on Spotify and selected about an hour of music for this prayer and healing service. This way, whoever joined us from around the world, would be listening to and worshipping to the same praise music as everyone else.

We also contacted some of our closer and trusted friends who know how to pray for the sick and then initiated the service. Some people would post their prayer notes directly to my page, and our friends who were helping us would take those requests and write a prayer back to the person who sent it. Jason and I had two laptop computers in the kitchen and would get private message notes, and we would each write out a prayer, stop, and pray it out loud. Then Diane would record the person, that person's location, and what the prayer request was about before we hit send.

Over the next seven to ten days, we received around sixty-five direct answers to prayer, with many complete healings at 100% and a few whose healings were in the process. It was fun as we met and prayed for people from around the world, many of whom we had never met before. All we did was take some courage and use technology to help us expand and advance the kingdom of God around the world from our small kitchen table. What a blessing it was to share and impart healing to others and see God work and move in their lives. We were grateful for the opportunity.

Journey

You've just read a bunch of true accounts in which people just like you took courage and stepped out of their comfort zones. They used the theology training that they had and added a theophany experience too. One of two scenarios is probably going through your mind right now. You might be thinking, *I could never do that*, or (and I hope this is the selection) you may be responding with some level of confidence and thinking, *Yeah, I can do that*.

Please recall my earlier story when I was reading the book *Intercessory Prayer* [14] by Dutch Sheets, and early in the book he made a comment that goes something like this: When you pray, "Thy kingdom come. Thy will be done," believe that it happens now, as opposed to sometime in the future. Do you remember that I read that comment silently to myself and then declared out loud, "I can do that"? That declaration was a courageous statement that launched this current healing ministry. What courageous statement do you need to make?

I have often shared that the kingdom of God is voice-activated and touch-imparted. God used His voice to create the earth. He then frequently tells us in Scripture to proclaim, say, tell, share, and talk about the kingdom.

Take a look at 2 Corinthians 8:12. "For if there is first a willing mind, it is accepted according to what one has, and not according to what one does not have." Don't tell God what you don't have; instead, tell Him what you do have. Don't say you don't have enough education; tell Him what you do have. Don't let Him know that you were born on the wrong side of the tracks, but rather proclaim what you do have. Stop telling Him that you don't know enough of the Bible; just share with Him what you do have. Quit telling Him that you are quiet and meek and can't talk to anyone, and begin to announce that God can use even a quiet person to share with someone else who is also quiet. Tell God what you do have. Believe it, and you can achieve it. A willing mind is one that is willing to yield. With the many testimonies in this chapter alone, you can definitely see how God brought an abundant yield back to those who simply yielded their courage factor to the Lord. Remember the television show *Fear Factor*? Let's change that to *The Courage Factor*.

Spend some time in prayer right now and repent of the excuses you have given God over the years, asking Him to empower you with a spirit of boldness. I believe if you are sincere, He will answer that prayer. In a very short time, you will be totally amazed at what God is now doing in your life.

It was John F. Kennedy who authored the book *Profiles in Courage*. Let it be known that your spiritual DNA and personal profile is filled with courage for the kingdom of God. George W. Bush wrote a book called *A Charge to Keep*, which is based on a hymn by Charles Wesley in which he penned these words:

> A charge to keep I have, a God to glorify,
> A never dying soul to save, and fit for the sky.
> To serve the present age, my calling to fulfill;
> O may it all my powers engage, to do my Master's will.

First Corinthians 4:2 sets the standard with these words: "Moreover it is required of stewards to be found faithful." Faithfulness to the call! Faithfulness to the standard, and faithfulness to the employment of the kingdom. If not now, then when? If not you, then who? The Marines have a slogan: *Semper Fi*. The definition of this phrase is "Always Faithful"!

It's time! Be courageous!

Chapter Thirteen

There Goes One

YOU may remember back in chapter one where Harris was writing about his experience at a conference where I was speaking. He and his wife had gone forward to receive a touch from God, and he heard me proclaim, "There goes one," as his wife fell to the floor under the power of God. Now this particular biblical manifestation is not mentioned a lot in the Bible, but it has happened in the Old and New Testament. You may remember that in the Old Testament there are passages about when the priests would go into the temple to minister unto the Lord, but they could not stand because of the glory of the Lord (see 2 Chron. 5:14, KJV).

In the New Testament, we see that this manifestation happened when the guards came to arrest Jesus, asking where Jesus was (see John 18:6). Jesus responded, identifying Himself. At that point, the guards all fell over backwards. Keep in mind, this was NOT something that they would do voluntarily, possibly allowing a potential prisoner to escape, as the guards most likely would be punished with death. However, in both cases when some people get close to the Lord or in His presence, they simply can't stand because of the weightiness and glory of the Lord.

It's kind of hard to explain what happens if you have never experienced it firsthand yourself, but it is definitely a theophany moment: Bible teaching with Bible experience. So I am going to share some of the times I have personally experienced both in my own life by falling under the power and presence of the Lord, and when I have prayed for others and it happened to them too. By the way, in some circles, this is labeled as being "slain in the Spirit." But I personally do not like that term because *slain* implies death, and my experience has always been one of being more alive in the Spirit as a result of this manifestation.

It requires faith to believe that God wants to and can do something significant through this particular action. Remember, Harris shared that he felt something heavy leaving his chest and later discovered that his long bout of many years suffering with asthma was suddenly healed. I am so glad he and his wife decided to stay for the conference.

What a blessing it is to discover how God can move in our lives even in new and sometimes strange experiences, or at least in unfamiliar uncharted waters where our previous experience and familiarity about God could easily overshadow and dismantle the new thing God is doing if we aren't careful. People often miss God by just those few inches between their hearts and their minds. Robert Schuller used to say, "Inch by inch, everything is a cinch." 'Tis true with so much of the kingdom and manifestations too. Taking baby steps forward and toward what God is doing is a great and powerful way to truly learn at the Master's feet as a kingdom apprentice.

I remember the first time I saw it happen. I was in the balcony helping with some music at our Lutheran church in Charleston, South Carolina. A visiting pastor from a Lutheran Church in North Carolina was ministering that day, and during communion, he apparently stopped to pray for someone and they fell over backwards, displaying such divine peace and tranquility. I remember saying to myself, "I want to be able to do that someday." Little did I know that walking into that realm would definitely cost me something that I did not yet fully comprehend spiritually nor understand naturally. In fact, every new realm of God that I have embraced and traveled into has cost me. Sometimes, it has cost me dearly. I don't mean that it was negative, because every manifestation or display of God's kingdom has been a marvelous experience, but it has surely cost me some friends and brought me lots of criticism, with false blog posts condemning me, and on it goes. But I count it all as loss for the knowing of Jesus and His resurrection power in my life. It's always worth it in the long run, but it's still costly too.

A couple of years later I was living and ministering in Texas and had attended a Lutheran conference with my wife in San Antonio, where an up-and-coming preacher was making a presentation. This preacher called for those who wanted a touch from God to come forward. So, like Harris in chapter one, I went forward, except somehow I ended up in the middle of a very long line in this very large convention center room. People began to fall to my left and to my right, and when it was all said and done, I was the only one left standing. Unlike Harris, who is not very tall, I am 6' 7" and was an obvious standout in the middle of all those who fell under the power of God, including the hundreds of people who were either still in their seats or waiting to come up for their touch from God too. I was definitely embarrassed and couldn't wait to get back to my seat. I knew this was real, but I was not experiencing it and was frustrated, obviously in a limelight that I did not care to be in at that particular moment.

However, there must have been some impartation because as I went home to our church in Houston and began to pray for people, they too began to fall, and that was cool. I learned early on that God does not like it when we play with His anointing, and I did that for a very short season. I watched others that apparently also had this gift and sometimes mimicked them in their way of doing things, but God brought gentle correction to my life, and I learned to be who I am with what He has given me. Because of my height, I have discovered ways to move away from being intimidating and to help make people feel safe.

Before I go on, I want to share with you, my reader, that I really don't care if people fall, laugh, cry, shake or quack like a duck. What I truly care about is that either the people who received prayer or their pastor sends me an email a few days or weeks later and shares the fruit that is now developing in their lives as a result of the prayer ministry and possible manifestations that may also have accompanied the prayer ministry. I truly want to hear about fruit, growth, and new life that blossoms forth in the lives of those I pray for.

As I would pray for people, more and more people began to fall down under the apparent power of God. What was surprising was that I was praying for many people who had pain in their bodies, such as in their backs or necks and other extremities, and they would get up off the floor totally healed and well, with no pain. To my natural mind, this made no sense. How could a person with back pain fall to the floor, even with a catcher, lay on a hard floor—or even one with carpet—for an extended length of time and then get up and be totally pain free? This was definitely a shift into a whole new paradigm for me. But God was in it. Surely the devil would not want to heal people so that they could be more effective for Jesus by living without pain.

I remember once when I prayed for two pregnant ladies who were actually sisters, and I had them sit down on opposite ends of a couch as I prayed for them. They both simultaneously fell inward toward the center of the couch and just enjoyed the presence of the Lord. God was so gentle with both of those ladies, and as I recall, one of them was having complications with the pregnancy, and she was healed during the gentle moment on the couch. Wow, what a fantastic God we serve! Over the years, I have seen hundreds healed while falling during prayer, but at this juncture in my life, it was all new to me. It was simply the anointing coming on a person to manifest God's presence in a way that I guess could not happen any other way, or at the very least in a way that God chose to operate. Since it is His deal, then it is His way of doing things that we must respond to. It's called yielding.

Once while attending a pastoral conference, a pastor's wife approached me and publicly stated that she had never fallen under God's power, although she believed in it. I responded and told her that it would happen the next day. Sure enough, after my sharing and preaching time, I offered some prayer ministry. Up she came to the front, and down she went. It was glorious, as she described it. Just a perfect harmony with God at that moment.

Once at a home group in Houston, there was a large crowd. I began to pray for people, and many fell and were enjoying special times with Jesus. Some were laughing, while others were at rest and peace, seemingly in the arms of Jesus. Across the large living room was a bulky kind of man who was a Houston police officer, and I asked him if he wanted what so many others in the room were experiencing. He responded, "Yes." I then told him I could not get to him because of the press of the crowd and the number of people in the room, many of whom were on the floor. So, I just waved my arm at him and said, "Receive the Holy Spirit," and he immediately crumpled to the floor. Now, you know that if this was not legit, that no police officer is just going to fall to the floor. He later stated that it was like a pleasant weight came on him and he just could not stand. That's the presence of the Lord, just like the priests in the Old Testament experienced too.

A similar experience happened at a church in Columbus, Ohio, where I was invited to come for a Wednesday evening and share and pray for people. When I got done praying and was leaving the building, sometime around 11:45 p.m., there was a man in the foyer, a rugged-looking cowboy type, with strong arms, and wearing a cowboy hat and boots. He approached me for prayer but stated that he was not going to fall down like all of those other folks had.

I then asked him what else he didn't want God to do for him. He asked, "What do you mean?" I responded by sharing with him that he had already decided that God was not going to put him on the floor like some of the others. Therefore, he should tell me what else he did not want God to do for him so I would know how to pray more effectively.

He responded by saying, "Well ... I guess He could if He wants to."

To this I said, "I think He does." Then I asked, "Do you want a touch from God?" and he just nodded his head yes. So, I literally snapped my fingers and said, "Receive the Holy Spirit," and immediately he fell to the floor with no catchers and began laughing hysterically. My host and I waited for nearly fifteen minutes before he got up, rather inebriated and wobbly, saying that was better than any drug or any high he had ever had, and that Jesus was real.

I asked him if he wanted to experience God again in this way, and he shouted, "Yeah, man!" So I snapped my fingers, and he fell to the floor, laughing once again. My host and I left. For all I know, he could still be there laughing at this very moment. Did I mention this was at a mainline denominational church again? Incredible!

When I first came to pastor the rural church in Kansas, I just assumed that the previous pastor had taught on these things, but later learned from my apostolic oversight that this was not the case. So, I launched a series of teachings on the Holy Spirit, including one on this particular manifestation. When I had concluded the message, I brought all those forward who wanted to experience God in this way, but forgot to explain to them that there might be other manifestations. Thus, I began to explain some of those as well, when all of a sudden, a lady named Cindy suddenly fell without a catcher and hit her head on the chair behind her with a very loud crash. It startled all of us, but the amazing thing is that she got up later stating that she never felt anything hit her head and that she had no pain. Cindy is a friend to this day.

One time in a small town in central Ohio, I was ministering at a church that had just completed its new building and was not even dedicated yet. But I had been invited to come and minister, so we were all in this new building. However, the carpet had not yet been laid, so as I went to pray for people, a line formed in front of a row of chairs, and there was a person acting as a catcher for the first person whom I would pray for. Sure enough, that person fell, and the usher helped the individual gently down to the floor.

What we did not anticipate or see coming was that everyone else in line fell too. It was kind of like dominoes falling, except as the power hit each person, they fell backwards, rather than sideways. Remember, there was no carpet, and all the rest fell without an usher or catcher, landing squarely on the cement. No one was hurt, no one remembered hitting the pavement, and all stood up, proclaiming what a great experience it was to be with God in this way.

I share these experiences with you not to convince you, but simply to help you understand that lots of things God does are not things we would do, and in the natural they make no sense to us. In the natural, it makes no sense that the God of the universe would come, live, and inhabit our very own bodies and lives, or that we can simply proclaim healing or lay our hands on the sick and they will get well. That doesn't make a lot of natural sense either, but it happens all the time to me and to many others.

Just a few more stories for those who like stories. I remember one time, while serving as a pastor in rural Kansas, we had a leader who was giving us some problems in the church, and I really did not know how to handle the situation. I had prayed and prayed but was not getting the wisdom I needed, nor did I see according to John 5:19 what the Lord was doing in this situation.

One evening we went to hear a speaker at a church in a neighboring town, and I went up for prayer ministry. After some prayer, I was suddenly on the floor, enjoying the presence of God and having some good conversation, when suddenly the Lord began to download to me and show me what I had to do with this particular leader. It was really incredible. As I laid there on the floor, God was speaking to me and showing me how to solve the problem. Sometimes, when we are on the floor, it is as if we are so low that the only position we have is to look up, and God came through big time. I went back to our church, shared what the Lord had told me with our elders, they agreed that it was a good word from the Lord, and we implemented the ideas and strategies. It literally solved the problem for us as I suspected it would because God was in it, even when I was on the floor.

I like what Steve Hill used to say at the Pensacola revival when asked why people would fall. He would simply respond, "Because they could not stand." And that's the truth. However, sometimes the opposite is true too.

I was ministering in East Moline, Illinois, and as I was praying for people, a lady in the back of the room said something loud enough for everyone to hear, including me. She blurted this out: "Well, he doesn't have much power, because no one is falling." I will never forget it. Since everyone heard it, I decided to address the comment using the words of Jesus when He said it is an evil and adulterous generation that seeks a sign. Like I previously wrote, my goal is not to see the sign, but to see the fruit.

Let me say it this way: I am not as interested in the manifested sign as I am in the One Who actually manifested the sign. We should not seek the healing, but the Healer. Let's not go after the salvation, but rather the One Who gives us the salvation. Seeking the provision is not nearly as good as seeking the Provider. We need to get our priorities straight too. I am not crazy about churches that have lots of manifestations like falling and laughter in the building, but no one is changed; and there is no evangelism, no outreach, and definitely no growth from the experience with God. If all they have is a party-like atmosphere without spiritual growth and holiness coupled with biblical achievement, then something is definitely wrong.

I was teaching and sharing in Des Moines and felt led to pray for all of the leaders in the church. Each one came forward, and literally every one of the leaders fell down under God's power. Then a little petite lady came forward, and she literally gave me a three-minute sermon in front of everyone else declaring why she was not going to fall, why she did not believe in it, and why it was not in the Bible. When she was finished, all I did was give a slight hand gesture, just turning my hand over and simply responding, "Okay." I did not argue with her, try to persuade her, or even point to the rest of the leaders still on the floor. I just said, "Okay."

As soon as I said, "Okay," she crumpled to the floor and was glued there for the rest of the service. When the service finally ended, several others were trying to get her to stand up, but she could not get up, so we had to have three men actually carry her out to the foyer where they placed her on the couch until she was able to get up on her own. You might ask, "What happened?" All I can say is that God has His way.

Would God do that? Have you read the New Testament lately? Do you remember another doubter of the faith? In fact, he was more than a doubter; he was an accuser, and God had His way with him too on the road to Damascus. Yes, this was after the Cross too. There are other examples in the New Testament as well. But let's keep our focus here on what God is doing, not so much on what He is not doing. That has to be our model as we embrace what He is doing and not what He is not doing. I take this stance at every healing service I lead. Again, John 5:19 has to be our standard and model.

Three more: Are you up for them? One was in California where I was ministering to a bunch of youth at an Assembly of God church that had a growing youth ministry. Many of the guys rode skateboards to church, and they were all parked in the foyer. After I taught and shared one evening, I began to pray for many of those there. Prior to this, seventeen youth and students accepted the Lord that night, and most of them had never been in church before, had no clue what Christian television is, and had never seen any manifestation in a church before. So, as I began to pray for these young people, and some fell to the floor, the newer ones stood off to the side with eyes as big as saucers, taking it all in.

The senior pastor's daughter actually fell that evening too, and she was healed of some disease in her side when the pain completely vanished while she was lying on the floor. At one point, I turned to those watching, with some of them being big teenagers, football-type, lineman-size, if you know what I mean. I asked them if they wanted to experience what was going on in the room. Most nodded yes, so I backed away from them up to about twelve feet away and then prayed and asked God to touch them. One by one, they fell to the floor. Later, as they got up, they kept asking their friends how I was able to run over to them, pray for them in person, and then back away so quickly and still be across the room from them. Of course, their friends assured them that I had stayed in my place and position at least twelve feet away from them, but they could not believe it. When the pastor's daughter got well, they finally acknowledged that this was a God thing and they wanted more of God. In fact, there was a lot of food prepared to eat in another room. Yet hardly any youth wanted to leave the worship center to go eat, but instead preferred to stay in God's presence. Without knowing the precise Scripture verse, they were actually tasting and seeing that God was good.

That's what the manifestations should always do. They should draw people closer to Jesus, and that's my goal. If you have seen or experienced abuses elsewhere or had people try to push you over, I am sincerely sorry. Often, I don't even touch people, so as not to give the impression of pushing. I want everyone to have a genuine experience with God. One time at a local church in the Omaha area, I was ministering to children as a guest, and we had 107 kids on the floor all at the same time, just enjoying themselves with God and having fun with Jesus. It's okay to have fun with Jesus. These children were so engaged in what God was doing, and I heard comments from the parents for several weeks about how this ministry touched and changed lives at home. The parents knew it was genuine when the attitudes, responses, and actions of their children had changed, simply from resting on the floor with Jesus. Wow, is that cool or what?

My last story on this subject is about a friend of mine who came to a local church to hear me. We kind of knew each other then, but not really well. I was teaching about the anointing of God. There were a lot of people in the room, and during prayer time, I was moving from one person to another. Many were falling and having an experience with God. I prayed for this man who is now my friend. His name is Terry, and he did not fall, although he did experience a touch from God. But in his mind, as I began to move to the next person, he began to doubt whether any of this was legitimate. Suddenly, I stopped praying for the next person and went back to Terry and spoke to him without knowing what he was thinking, challenging him not to doubt just because he did not fall. I went on to declare that falling on the floor was not the ultimate, but falling more in love with God was. He smiled and then fell to the floor too, later sharing with me and everyone else in the room what you have just read. Terry is a great photographer, and this image is photographed in his mind to this day.

God knows what is going on in our lives, and He has ways of getting our attention. So, when Harris said in the opening chapter, "There goes one," it was God's way of getting his attention too, as his wife was the first to fall of the two to three hundred people who came forward at that conference in Minneapolis. How is God trying to get a hold of your attention today? Let's press on for more of Him in the Journey below. Remember, the steps of righteous people are ordered by the Lord. It's time to take another step.

Journey

This one is just between you and God. Ask Him now if what I am saying is true. Ask Him to show you how He may want you to experience something new simply by yielding. Will it be worth it? I believe it will. Will it cost you something? I believe it will.

This is a journey that is always costly and always worth it. Remember, it's not so much about falling over on the floor as it is about falling more in love with God. But if falling on the floor helps you fall more in love with God, then I would suggest that it is worth it.

Maybe God is asking you to do something else right now that will cost you. Are you willing to pay the price? Let me state it a different way. Are you willing to *pray* the price? There is a price to be prayed with every new step and direction God takes us. I urge you to set your heart on things above and pursue what God is asking you to do, even if it makes you uncomfortable.

I like what Bill Johnson has said when asked, "Where is this in the Bible?" His response is that Psalm 115 says God does what He pleases. The Bible reveals His nature but does not contain Him or set boundaries for Him.

Check it out in Psalm 115:3.

Then, Mike Bickle from the Kansas City International House of Prayer was quoted with this good thought-provoking consideration: "God will offend the mind to reveal the heart."

Chapter Fourteen

Getting Un-Tongue Tied

THIS could be a challenging chapter for you if you have not experienced praying in the Spirit. Perhaps you have even taken a theological stance that is radically opposed to praying in the Spirit, but I truly want you to move past the personal theology and read with an open mind. For many years, my theology, but not my theophany, included praying in the Spirit or speaking in tongues. I simply stated that others had those gifts and I did not. I later learned that all of the gifts of the Spirit are available for all believers at any time, even though each of us will possess and flow in at least one or several specific gifts given to us to edify the body of Christ and release freedom to others while simultaneously advancing the Kingdom of God. Paul says it well in Colossians 1:27, stating that the ministry (including the gifts) was given to us to fulfill the word of God.

Remember, theology without theophany is like reading your Bible without experiencing the truth of it. We need both good theology and good theophany. I will attempt to offer both, although briefly, in this one chapter.

The main point is that over and over as I and others would yield to this special and unique gift, we would see a yield return to us in amazing and transforming ways that simply promoted the teachings of the New Testament writers as their words came alive in our lives. This happens today with ongoing anointing and transforming power that only God can do throughout the ages because He is alive in each generation, actively moving, teaching, and demonstrating His purposes and agenda to expand the kingdom of God here on earth.

Let's begin first with a Scripture verse from several translations. Jude 1:20, in the New King James Version, says, "But you, beloved, building yourselves up on your most holy faith, praying in the Holy Spirit." In the

Message Bible, it reads like this: "But you, dear friends, carefully build yourselves up in this most holy faith by praying in the Holy Spirit." Then, from the Amplified Bible, we see these words: "But you, beloved, build yourselves up, [founded] on your most holy faith [make progress, rise like an edifice higher and higher] praying in the Holy Spirit." Finally, from the Voice: "You however, should stand firm in the love of God, constructing a life within the holy faith, praying the Spirit's prayer."

Praying in the Spirit seems to be an important and integral part of keeping our faith strong, active, alive, and flowing. Let me explain this a bit further to help bring some understanding. We often find ourselves praying for something in our lives or the lives of people we know, and while we believe in prayer and the power of prayer, sometimes we don't see the answer coming as fast as we might expect or anticipate. And sometimes, when this is prolonged over an extended timeframe, we could lose our hope. Consequently, our faith begins to diminish or drain down to an unhealthy level in this particular area. If your heart rate drops too low in the natural, it can prove to be an unhealthy environment for you. This applies to our faith too. The Bible says that we go from faith to faith, but the implication is that faith is adding more faith to the previous amount that we had, not disintegrating or spiraling downward.

Therefore, we may have lots of faith in other areas, while we simultaneously seem to be losing ground in this one prayerful area. What I have learned from the Word of God and through great teaching from others is that as I pray in my native tongue, which for me is obviously English, I do so with faith, joy, and anticipation. But if I don't see an answer and have not heard from the Lord, my faith sometimes will bottom out or wane in the process. If I am not careful, discouragement will come in and replace the faith completely, and I can easily give up. If this happens, I end up yielding to the discouragement rather than to what God has instructed me to do. I suspect you have done this a time or two in your life.

The Bible tells us that if I pray in the Spirit, I will edify or build up or construct a life of faith that can and will see me through during those tough prayer times, or difficult and trying times in my life. You may have prayed for something one hundred times, and when you began to pray the first time, your faith was strong and active. But later, after a few days or weeks, it seems that you can barely utter a word. At this point, you have to switch from your native tongue and begin to pray in the Spirit. Your faith may have decreased a little or a lot, but by extended praying in the Spirit, your faith will rise, and at some point, you can then switch back over to your native tongue and pray in faith once again. It is powerful and incredibly true. Let me share a story to illustrate.

In the year 2000, my family and I moved from Dallas to Omaha, where Diane and I were employed at a local church and school. Our son Jason was in third grade at the time, and he received free tuition in the school as a part of the financial package. Diane was a teacher, and I was the school administrator. My job description included restarting the contemporary Spirit-filled service at this church that they had previously enjoyed three years prior. The pastoral office and position had also been vacant for three years.

We had a great year and started some amazing programs in the school, and God was working in the school in so many ways. We initiated a Bible study in our home to begin to launch the contemporary service. In the school, we had children praying for each other and for guests, as well as witnessing and sharing the power of God. Healings were frequent, and God was working in really incredible ways.

Suddenly, without much warning, and through a lot of religious and ungodly maneuvering and manipulation from an outside source, a new pastor was brought on board. He began to dismantle so many things that we and many others before us had initiated. As a result, the school closed, and all seventeen employees lost their jobs on the same day, including staff from the elementary and high school. Diane and I were the only couple on staff, so it was doubly hard, as you can imagine.

Diane had applied at a local Assembly of God school and was hired provisionally, with the state of Nebraska saying that she could work but would have to complete two courses to satisfy the state's teaching requirements. She had a whole year to do this, and I began to travel and minister outside of the area as God would open the doors.

Shortly after, and just prior to school starting, the state came back and said that they had made a mistake and that Diane would have to complete these two courses prior to actually teaching at this school. So, she had to let the school administrator know this and basically had to let the job go while she enrolled in two fall classes through a local college. It was a tough season for us, as my income was very limited, Diane had no income, and we were also home-schooling our son Jason in fourth grade at the time.

Through prayer and much perseverance, Diane completed the courses, and then one of the teachers at the Assembly of God school got pregnant. So, Diane was hired in the middle of the school year for that position, which she held for eleven years until that school also closed in the spring of 2012.

In the meantime, in 2001 I was invited to have a phone interview with a rather large Spirit-filled Methodist church in Orlando, Florida. I am originally from San Diego and love the tropical weather, frequently being able to wear shorts, Hawaiian shirts, and flip flops year-round, so this opportunity was very appealing. As it turned out, I was invited to go on an interview for the teaching pastor position. Not only was the job description everything I loved to do, but it also included a laptop, cell phone, three weeks of vacation for our family, and three weeks of missions work or intentionally advanced education, plus a teaching job for Diane, moving expenses, health insurance for the family, and free tuition in their school for Jason through high school. The total package was $110,000 walking in the door, and we had been without steady income now for about seven months. Did I mention it was in Orlando? I did, didn't I?

Think of the comparison: a nice warm climate, lots of entertainment value in Orlando, with great job descriptions and salary versus our home in Omaha, limited income, and lots of snow that year piled up way too high for this California boy. We began a quest to secure prayer, and I got together with fifteen local pastors that I knew in Omaha, asking them to pray. Every one of them thought that I should turn the position down, yet none of them offered us a dime to stay. Still, that is what they concluded, and to be honest, we were also leaning toward turning this position down as well. It was a tough choice, for sure. From the outside, it looked like a great position and a fantastic opportunity, but still we turned it down and felt like we had heard from God.

Just a few weeks later, Diane was at school teaching and Jason had been accepted into fourth grade there as well; but I was at home alone, the snow was piled up higher, and I had absolutely no speaking engagements set up for the remainder of the year 2001. I was frustrated, cold, depressed, and was thinking hard about the decision we had made. Did I mention that the job offer was in Orlando? Do you remember reading that?

Here I was at home lamenting (that's a good biblical and spiritual term for grumbling and complaining) when I remembered something a local pastor had preached in a message: "You can't pray in the Spirit and stay depressed." So I thought, okay, I will give it a try.

I began to pray in the Spirit or other tongues. To be honest, I had to yield my personal tongue to do this, because while I believed the local pastor, I was stuck at home with no income, in a cold climate, wishing I was in Orlando, and really having a tough time with not providing for my family and not supporting us financially the way I thought it should be accomplished. Initially, my prayer language, or tongue, was very weak. It probably sounded like shoe, shoe, shimmee, shimmee, shimmee, shoe. And if interpreted, we might have heard something like, "See Spot run. See Spot walk. See Spot crawl. See Spot exhausted." It was very weak tongues without much gusto, faith, or feeling at all. But I kept at it.

Before I continue, I need to explain and state that a prayer language is different from the gift of tongues. I may have had the gift of tongues once in my life, but I think I chickened out and did not give the message. You see, prophecy is a message from God in a known language and tongues is a message from God in an unknown language. But in this account and story, I am referring to an actual prayer language that 1 Corinthians 14 talks about. Now, let's proceed with the story.

I recall that after twenty minutes my prayer language was much stronger, at forty minutes I was up walking around the house and praying loudly, and at sixty minutes, I was shouting, and the city was mine. Nothing had changed in the natural or on the outside. The snow was still high, and I did not have any income, but on the inside I was supercharged and ready to conquer whatever the enemy would throw at us. My faith had grown, developed, and risen to a new level in those sixty minutes. It was an incredible journey of faith expansion, created simply by applying the Scriptures, yielding to God, and seeing Him work supernaturally in my life, while bringing a yield back to me as well.

A postscript is that I watched that Orlando church for several years, and they actually had four different people in that position over five years, including the senior pastor's wife. Then suddenly, that pastor left the church and there was some upheaval and lingering disunity as a result. I was so glad that I had turned that position down. It was a God-decision and a God-affirmation later in the one hour prayer time. It was powerfully anointed too.

At the conclusion of Mark 16, in this amended section of the Great Commission, we are told that one of the things that will accompany the believers is that they will speak with new tongues. Now, some theologians and churches contend that this chapter of the Bible was never in the original manuscript, and to be honest, we have no way of knowing. But whenever people bring that up, I ask them why they have not ripped that chapter out of their Bible if they don't believe it is true.

Even some of the more well-known theologians and pastors of our time have preached sermons and written books about this subject in Mark 16, and some of them have even published Bibles with their names on it. Yet, they left this chapter in their personal edition to be sold. Doesn't that seem strange to you? It is even stranger than turning down a position in warm Orlando. Okay, enough of that.

Mark 16:17 says that these signs will follow those who believe, and then they are listed for us. I won't take time to list the whole passage here, as you can read it on your own. I have often wondered why some of my good friends who have a solid relationship in Jesus, love the Lord, and believe in His word, along with the power of the resurrection, don't see, expect, or experience these signs. Let me restate it to ask it in this manner: I have wondered why they don't or can't yield to these signs.

Let me share what I think has happened and rephrase verse seventeen just a bit more to bring some understanding. These signs will follow those who *believe* these signs will follow. Some of my friends simply don't believe that these signs will follow, so the signs don't follow them. It's that simple. But for those who will believe, what an astounding and miraculous journey awaits them! New opportunities that would have frustrated them in the past can now be opened, attained, accomplished, and achieved by the prevailing power and presence of the Holy Spirit simply by yielding and believing.

Matthew 21:22 says, "Whatsoever things you ask in prayer, believing, you will receive." I must conclude that, while I have friends with a strong relationship with Jesus, they have not believed for these signs to follow them; therefore, they don't. Matthew 22:29 states that we are in error if we don't embrace the Scriptures and the power of God. There is definite power in the Scriptures, but there seems to be even more power available to us through the Holy Spirit. Thus, while Jesus knew the Scriptures and the power that was in those Scriptures, He was also anointed with power by the Holy Spirit. In fact, when Jesus was twelve years old, He was using those Scriptures to talk to the leaders in the temple, but He never did anything miraculous or supernatural until He was anointed with power from and through the Holy Spirit at His baptism.

The separation from the natural to the spiritual and then linked back to the natural through this simple yet profound gift is astonishing and prodigious that produces a vast amount of faith and power to consummate the current or next task. New unity in the faith through the power of the Holy Spirit is exhilarating when walking in that position, but your life can be severely frustrating when you are unable to attain and gain the progress needed because your faith has declined. God has provided a way for those low faith times not to become long, lingering times of difficult wondering that causes some to wander away from the truth, but instead to commence times that promote great understanding and increased faith values that then carry us over the next hurdle, the next wave, or the next obstacle.

I like what Psalm 18:28–29 says: "For You will light my lamp; The Lord my God will enlighten my darkness. For by You I can run against a troop, by my God I can leap over a wall." Everyone would agree that oil was needed to light lamps in those days, and the obvious connection here is that the strength and power needed to overcome these obstacles would be the anointing power of the Holy Spirit. Isaiah 10:27 declares that the anointing destroys the yokes of bondage. Some translations say the yoke is broken because of the anointing, but if something is merely broken, it might be able to be fixed, repaired, and put back together. However, when something is destroyed, there are not enough pieces left to reassemble it. This is what God wants to do with the power of the Holy Spirit in our lives.

A few years ago, while leading a healing service at a church in the Omaha area, we were praying for people with sore necks to be healed, and everyone in the room with that condition got well or had tremendous noticeable improvement, except for one young teenage girl who I believe was fifteen at the time. I remember that she was crying due to her pain, and we were using every prayer tactic we could think of that was given in the Bible. I am sure we missed a few, but we were sincerely trying, yet nothing was working.

Finally, I asked everyone just to stop and be quiet. I explained that I was going to pray in the Spirit and also shared where that was in the Bible and what I was actually going to do, because I believe that demonstration with explanation brings edification and eliminates confusion. So I began to pray quietly in the Spirit. I was praying aloud but not very loudly or demonstratively at all, when suddenly I knew what the answer was.

Through praying in the Spirit, I gained understanding, and wisdom flowed to me. The Bible says in 1 Corinthians 14:15, "I will pray with the spirit, and I will also pray with understanding." That word is also a promise from God that as I pray in the Spirit or with the Spirit, understanding will then begin to flow to me where I previously lacked understanding. The order of this passage is critical to our comprehension of what God is doing.

God did not instruct us with the words "I will pray with understanding and I will then pray with the Spirit." Some people want to understand everything before they do it, but that takes the faith element out of the equation. Some others want to question and comprehend every spiritual application in the Bible, and if they can't come up with a good reason in the natural, then they dismiss those biblical options as being something that was for a limited time and conclude that they no longer exist. They hold onto what they can explain, but where there is no explanation and one must accept it entirely by faith, then these things are often tossed out like old scraps of food on a dinner plate. It is ridiculous to take this position and miss all that God has for us. Let me finish the story.

As I was praying in the Spirit, I knew what the problem was, and I immediately stopped and asked the girl if her mother had a very sore neck. She said, "Yes." I then asked if her grandmother also had this neck problem, and she affirmed that as well. So, I simply broke the power of a generational curse, using the anointing of Isaiah 10:27, which says that the anointing shall destroy the yoke, as previously mentioned. Then, I gently touched her neck and declared healing. Instantly, her neck was totally well without any pain.

What happened? I accessed the power of God, and He brought an understanding to the situation that confounded even the greatest skeptics in the room as they saw this girl get well before our eyes. She stopped crying and was elated to receive healing from Jesus. Someone ought to be shouting about now! Come on, at least give me a good "amen" in your outside voice! You can do it. I know you want to. Don't be embarrassed. So what if others

Getting Un-Tongue Tied

might hear you? This might open up an opportunity to witness or pray for someone as you share why you just said "amen" to this wonderful and true story. If no one is in the room, then there is no reason not to shout, "Amen!"

Several years ago, I was invited to speak at a church in El Paso. Prior to accepting the offer to go there, the senior pastor called me and asked me to explain to him what I believed about all of the miraculous gifts of the Spirit. I took my time and went through each one, and he was convinced that I had a balanced theological approach and then confirmed that he wanted me to come there and minister.

So I journeyed to El Paso, and one of the services was designated as a healing service. Many people showed up from El Paso and also from across the border in Juarez, Mexico. One man came in on crutches, with his left leg bent up very awkwardly. As he hobbled in, everyone's eyes were on him. Later in the service, I had the opportunity to pray for his healing, but not much was happening. I asked him to sit down, and I had the pastor sit across from him while I sat on the side of the leg that was bent up.

I had the man stretch out his good leg to the pastor, and I began to pray for healing. At some point, I switched over to praying in the Spirit, or in tongues, and I really got after it. Shortly after I started, his leg literally began to uncurl, and within moments it was stretched out nearly straight but was still somewhat shorter than the other leg. I then commanded it to grow further out, but nothing happened. So, I went back to praying in tongues, and within a few minutes, the leg grew out the rest of the way to a normal length. It was once again of the most amazing things I had seen to that point in my life and ministry. The man jumped up and started running around the room, and the people were shouting and rejoicing as this man from Mexico without any kind of insurance had been healed by God. Wow, that was fantastic, for sure. I won't prompt you to shout this time, hoping that you are already doing it.

Later that evening, the pastor got mad at me. I asked what was wrong, and he said he was mad that I had prayed in tongues, and he was just livid about the whole experience. I finally asked him if he remembered our phone call when I explained what I believed and when he had responded at the time that it was all good. He did recall our conversation, but he honestly did not think I would implement any of the gifts of the Spirit, especially one so controversial.

I asked him how speaking in tongues was controversial and encouraged him to focus on what God had done and how the man got well, rejoicing in that and not being so concerned about what others might think. But of course, he went on about it for quite awhile, so I just remained quiet and prayed. Fortunately one of his leaders came over and shared how he also believed in praying in tongues and that he was always afraid to share it until now, so that seemed to calm the local pastor down. That leader never got into any trouble over it either. It was a glorious event with a strange ending.

There is another story that happened in conjunction with my trip to El Paso that I will share in the next chapter, and it too is just another example of how yielding to God brings a yield on the scene. What might have happened had I not prayed in the Spirit? I know that you might be thinking, *Well, the pastor would not have been so upset*, but beyond that I am thinking that the man on crutches might not have been healed either. I don't mind taking a little heat from others while I am following what God is doing. I am in good company and would rather see people get well and walk in freedom than try to keep everyone happy.

Jack Deere was on the faculty of Dallas Theological Seminary, but at some point in the 1980s had a Holy Spirit experience. I like what he once said. He stated that for many years he had made mistakes on the side of excessive death, so if he had to make a mistake, he would do it now on the side of excessive life. That is my position too. And I believe it is God's, as He clearly said that Jesus came that we might have life and life even more abundantly, but the enemy came to kill, rob, and destroy. Let me put it another way: God came to impart life to us, while the enemy came to try to make that life depart from us.

Years before that episode in El Paso, when I was on staff at a Lutheran church in the Houston area, my senior pastor and I attended a pastoral prayer time hosted by a local Hispanic church called *Igelsia Sobra de la Roca*, which translates to Church on the Rock. There was a good mix of Anglo pastors and Hispanic pastors who attended. Pastor Ken and I sat together when the prayer service began, and at some point everyone started praying in tongues. It was a special time, and I had been around Pastor Ken for a number of years and knew what his prayer language sounded like, so I could definitely tell he was praying in that language. I also knew what Spanish sounded like, as I had grown up in San Diego, had many Hispanic friends, and had taken some Spanish classes myself.

At one point, a number of Hispanic pastors approached Pastor Ken and began speaking to him rapidly in Spanish, all at the same time. It was a sight and really seemed important to these Hispanic pastors. Pastor Ken stopped them in English, waving his hands at them, saying, "Hold on, fellows! I don't understand a word of Spanish, so someone has to translate." These pastors did not believe him because they had just heard Pastor Ken praying in Spanish, a special prayer that was so vivid, authentic, and real for their current situation that they just knew it must be from God, since Pastor Ken had never met these Hispanic pastors.

I was there and can attest for sure that Pastor Ken was indeed praying in the Spirit, but these Hispanic pastors all heard it in Spanish, concluded that God had spoken to Pastor Ken about their situation, and were asking him to expand on what he had prayed. In the natural, Ken had not uttered one word in Spanish, and could not explain what he had prayed, yet the other pastors all heard it in Spanish. It was a supernatural moment. This was just so incredible and yet also very credible, as God had provided a Pentecost experience for those of us in the room, where others heard what was being spoken in their own language.

Are you getting any of this? Do you see the special significance of how God can use this gift to expand the kingdom if only we will yield to it and respond appropriately in a way that demonstrates we believe that these gifts will follow those who believe that these gifts exist?

Sometimes, when I go to churches that believe in and practice praying in the Spirit, I ask those folks to come forward who have basically had the same words or phrases for many years. I begin to pray over them, often touching their vocal chords and praying for an expansion of their prayer language. Many people get more and more words and phrases, while some go into warfare tongues and others more intercessory tongues, but it is such a joy for these people to be able to express back to God in new words and phrases. Just like children who grow up and learn more and more vocabulary words, so there is a greater language to learn in the spirit realm of the kingdom of God.

There are a number of passages in the Bible that speak about being mature and growing into maturity, yet some people remain immature because of their church doctrine when it comes to certain gifts of the Spirit, including tongues. I have been in services where gifted yet ignorant leaders tried to teach others to pray in the Spirit. Sometimes, they try to get the person who just prayed for the infilling of the Holy Spirit to mimic or say the same phrases that they are saying. There have been jokes about some of these phrases, such as repeating the words "economical condominium" over and over. Or my personal favorite, "Shin and knee, thigh, butt; shin and knee, thigh, butt." These are obviously not the way that God wants us to operate, and those who do these crazy things need to walk into some new levels of maturity. Tongues cannot be taught by human form. It is a gift from God and must be initiated from Him.

The problem is that some church doctrines teach that the first giving of the Holy Spirit in the New Testament was at Pentecost and included tongues, so everyone else must also follow that same pattern and understanding. These doctrines are not really fully accessing what the patterns of the Bible suggest. For instance, I often challenge folks who believe that the first expression or download of the Holy Spirit was at Pentecost. Actually, it was much sooner in the New Testament, when Elizabeth was filled with the Holy Spirit and began to prophesy to Mary while John was leaping in Elizabeth's womb. In this case, the demonstration or activation of the Holy Spirit was twofold and included prophecy with an unborn child leaping in the womb. If we aren't careful and take this literally, then the only people who can receive the Holy Spirit are women who are pregnant. That eliminates all men from ever receiving the Holy Spirit, along with all women who aren't pregnant. Most people would say that that is goofy or foolish, and I would challenge that the same mindset that insists tongues has to accompany the infilling of the Holy Spirit is also way off track.

I know many people who have been filled with the Holy Spirit and did not get a prayer language for many years. In one case, our pastor in South Carolina who introduced this to us had only the single syllable of "ah" for six months before God released more of a spiritual and heavenly language in him. He just yielded to that one syllable for all of those months until God brought the yield back to him. It's God's deal, so we need to take our hands off His dispenser and disperse what He wants.

I like what Chuck Smith (one of the founding leaders of the Calvary Chapel Movement) says in his book *Charisma vs. Charismania*.[15] He pens that the primary evidence of the Baptism of the Holy Spirit or the infilling of the Holy Spirit is that of love. *"We fall more in love with Jesus, and we love to worship him more, and our love for the kingdom increases"* (emphasis mine). It really does fit the overall pattern of the Bible much more concisely because all of the gifts of the Spirit as I understand them are given to glorify Jesus and to promote the kingdom, rather than centering in on one experience. But the gift of tongues and/or a prayer language is a valid expression for the church today, and we need to bypass all of the theological explanations and rhetoric and just yield to God to see what He wants to do. It really is that simple.

For my good theologically astute friends who do far more than simply discuss theological issues but actually get out and advance the kingdom, seeing people saved and healed through the Gospel, please forgive me, as I know your hearts are pure and your motives are sincere. But for the other groups of armchair theologians who just love to sit around and argue point after point, trying to justify certain positions while leaving shipwrecked people in their wake and making the Scriptures irrelevant for today, this next quote is for you. I have heard Jesse Duplantis say this, and it really can be true: "It takes a good theologian to help you misunderstand the Bible." Yes, I used this quote earlier in the book, but it bears repeating.

Please understand that as I share this next story about my life, it is just a reporting of what happened. There was a time when I was wounded and hurt because of this ordeal, but I am now well past that hurt and carry no pain nor open wound of any kind. Still, the impact and truth of the story is applicable and should be shared to help bring a deeper understanding and awareness of what God wants to do and can do in our lives if we will yield to Him, rather than just yielding to religious doctrines. The reality of the outcome, though very unpleasant at the time, actually yielded God's purpose in bringing us to Omaha from Dallas. Fruit was planted and is now being yielded, and God is working all things after His good pleasure. (Check out Ephesians 1:9 and Philippians 2:13.)[16]

When I was on staff as the school administrator at the inner city school that I wrote about earlier in this chapter, the new pastor came in and basically shut everything down. This was because he did not believe in the gifts of the Spirit for today. One of the first things he told me was that I needed to stop saying, "God said," because he believed that God only spoke through word and sacrament. So, I asked him how he decided to leave his last church and come to this location in Omaha. What Scripture verse did God use and/or how did God speak during the sacraments for him to sell his house and move his family to this location? I was not trying to be argumentative, but to learn about his position so I could represent him well to the parents of the school.

He could not answer me, but still held to his reply. He did tell me on several occasions, though, that pure doctrine was more important than people. Wow, I don't remember seeing that in the Bible. Jesus died for the people of the world, not the doctrines of the world. It was the religious crowd that Jesus agonized over and had the most trouble with, and it seems to be true today too.

I later learned that this pastor was a theologian with advanced degrees and was on the board of directors for his particular denomination. One day, he called me into his office for a discussion about the gifts of the Spirit. He told me in no uncertain terms that this particular denomination did not believe in the gifts of the Spirit and that I needed to stop testifying to others that God still worked this way.

I challenged him, stating that the opening paragraph of the handbook of the denomination stated explicitly that the denomination does indeed believe in the gifts of the Spirit as outlined in 1 Corinthians 12. Of course, he argued back that no such statement exists, but I kept my ground and continued to share in a very soft but firm voice that I believed it did.

He got his copy out and read it, then slammed it down on his desk and in a rather abrupt tone stated, "Well, that's what is says, but that is not what it means." Remember, it takes a good theologian to help you misunderstand the Bible. I think he meant well and was representing his denomination the best he knew how, but the reality is that God's Word is clear and it is true, without error.

It is imperative to remember that when the gifts were offered and shared in the Bible, it was with an eternal perspective. Everything God gives us is designed to last forever. His presence shall never leave us. Our callings are forever. The Word of God remains eternally. And there is no mention or place in the Bible where it says the gifts ceased. Why would you or anyone else want to believe otherwise? Why would we want to take what God wrote and try to make it say something else? Our intentions should be to trust God and proceed with His plan, which includes the gifts of the Spirit for today, and yes, even tongues.

Years ago, when I was on staff at a church in Texas, there was a lady who was battling cancer and had many trying and difficult medical procedures to endure. She went from one elder to another and one pastor to another in our growing church, asking for prayer for healing from this cancer. Within fourteen days of asking me to pray for her, she was in total remission. She often praised my prayer, but in reality, I think she went alphabetically, and I just got in on the tail end of some other great prayers by these other men of God in our church.

After she was pronounced well and free of cancer, she would approach me every week and ask for prayer that the cancer would not return. She was in such fear and anxiety, and I knew that this could not continue. At home, I prayed for her and asked the Lord for instructions on how to pray for her in the future. He told me to offer her the baptism of the Holy Spirit, or the infilling of the Holy Spirit, because she was so fearful. He said the power that would be released through this prayer would give her the courage she needed to overcome this fear from Sunday to Sunday. However, the Lord went on to tell me that if she would not receive the prayer for the baptism of the Holy Spirit, then I would not be allowed to pray for her ever again.

Well, this was a very serious word from God, so I went to our pastor and shared it with him for discernment. He felt that I had indeed heard from God. Sure enough, the next Sunday this lady came to me, asking for prayer to battle the fear that the cancer might come upon her once again. I then offered her the baptism of the Holy Spirit. She stopped me and said she did not want any of that Holy Spirit stuff because she did not want to fall on the floor, speak in tongues, or do any of that other stuff. All she wanted was prayer not to get cancer again. I then offered the infilling of the Holy Spirit to her again, but she repeated with the same response as before.

It was at this point that I told her that if she did not let me pray for the filling of the Holy Spirit in her life, then I would not be allowed to pray with her ever again, and that this had been affirmed by our pastor. She still declined and headed off to find someone else to pray for her. Ultimately, within just a few short months, the cancer came upon her. She passed away very quickly, and I never prayed for her again. To write about it pains me even now because I so wanted to pray for her, but God had given a word, and my pastor had confirmed it. I had to respond in obedience to both realms.

Job 3:25 says this: "The thing which I greatly feared has come upon me and what I dreaded has happened to me." I believe this lady could have avoided this, as God gave clear advice on how to eliminate this fear and walk in wholeness, while remaining healthy and cancer-free. But that which she feared came upon her. I have heard others say in response to this verse, "Fear God and let Him come upon you."

That's what it boils down to: letting the Holy Spirit come upon you and in you. I don't have room to teach you all of the interacting nuances of this subject, but the Holy Spirit is on you for others and in you for you. When you pray in the Spirit, this is one of those times that the Holy Spirit is in you to encourage and edify just you. But the result is that you carry the presence of the Holy Spirit to others, and the reason is to bless, encourage, help, and bring aid to others who need a kingdom touch.

You may be at a crossroads right now. On the one hand, you may have been taught, like I was, that the gifts of God have somehow stopped or ceased to exist. Yet, as you have read so much of this book to this point, you know that I am not exaggerating the truth and that the gifts of God are at work in my life and in the lives of so many others through the reports and stories you have digested to this point.

Then again, you may be simply at a point where you know that it is time for you to yield to God in this realm, even with limited understanding, but respond in faith and move on with what God has for you. It's your choice. The Bible states in Acts 10:34 that God is not a respecter of people. In other words, what He will do for one, He will do for another. But He is a respecter of choices. Throughout the Bible He gives us choice after choice in so many areas and about so many aspects of life. Whatever choice we make, He will honor. He does not beat His kids, nor does He manipulate, dominate, or intimidate them, forcing them to do it His way. It's your choice. Will you yield to Him in this area or skip over it to the next chapter and maybe deal with it another time?

What will be your choice?

Journey

This one will be pretty simple. Just pray right now and ask God to clear your mind. Then ask Him to fill you with His Spirit, or to re-fill you, as Ephesians 5:18 says to keep on being filled with the Spirit. Then, wait and see what happens.

I believe God will answer that prayer very quickly, and you will experience something. You will have a theophany. That theophany will then qualify your theology. I believe you will have a theophany moment that will bless and encourage you for a lifetime. At the very least, a fresh anointing will come on you from the Holy Spirit, and you will know that something new is happening in your life. Psalm 92:10 speaks about being anointed with fresh oil, or having a fresh anointing. I don't want to put thoughts or patterns into your mind presently. I only desire that you have an encounter with God. But I do challenge you to yield to Him in this process. I believe you will be glad you did.

As previously stated, when we were first offered these options, our greatest fear was that of losing friends. I did lose one pastor friend to this day who will not talk to me, but I gained thousands of other new friends. The number one reason given in the Bible not to fear is because God is with you. Let me say it again: God is with you. Don't be afraid. Remember the passage in Job, but please don't go that direction. Instead, if you are going to fear something or anything at all, then fear God and let Him come upon you. I believe you will be glad you did.

You can pray on your own or simply pray this prayer out loud: "Holy Spirit, I invite Your presence into my life right now. And Lord, I thank you for this chapter that I just read. I really do want the Holy Spirit to fill me, come upon me, touch me, and change me. Jesus, I thank You for sending Your Holy Spirit to us to do these very things. So right now, I ask that the Holy Spirit would fill me, baptize me, come upon me, and change me. I wait expectantly for how the Spirit may want to manifest in me, but I believe that new power is coming to me right now, and my life will never be the same, in the name of Jesus. Amen."

Chapter Fifteen

Study Time: Part 5

I mentioned in the last chapter that I had another story to share revolving around my El Paso trip, so I am launching with that story here because it fits the theme of this chapter so well. Galatians 6:7 states that whatever a person sows he will reap. I believe that is true and often see it in my life and that of my family, along with others who I know believe this principle too. Remember, the primary reason that the various gifts listed in Mark 16 happen today is because someone understands God's Word and actually believes what it says. For those who don't believe, these kinds of manifestations and actions from God don't materialize in their lives.

Prior to traveling to El Paso, I was checking out in a grocery store, and there was a Hispanic man behind me who had placed three boxes of fried chicken, a loaf of French bread, and some bottles of soda on the conveyor belt. I decided to strike up a conversation with him, and I discovered that he was from Guatemala and that he was pouring cement at a new shopping center nearby. He was in the store to purchase lunch for himself and two friends.

As we were waiting for the cashier to scan my items, I asked how he liked Omaha. He kind of paused and was reticent, but I encouraged him to tell me the truth. So he proceeded to tell me that sometimes the police would profile the Hispanic community and that some businesses in the warehouse industry would overwork the migrant workers, making them work for seven days, but only paying them for six.

As this conversation was continuing, I noticed that most of my groceries had now been scanned, so I offered to pay for this man's food as well. He was reluctant, but he agreed. It only came to about fifteen to twenty dollars or so. He asked me why I wanted to buy his groceries, and I simply responded that

I wanted him to know that not all Anglos would treat him badly in Omaha and that I welcomed him to our community. As we walked out of the store together, I then shook his rough, cement-covered hand and asked him if he had found a church yet, thinking that he might be Catholic. He said that he had been looking but had not found the right Pentecostal church to attend that was also fluent in Spanish. I was able to make two recommendations to him of local Hispanic churches that might be a good fit for him, neither of which he had heard of.

Then three days later I arrived in El Paso and was checking in at my hotel. I had booked a room in a local Holiday Inn, and as I was signing the necessary paperwork with the desk clerk, another man approached me from behind the counter and asked if I was the Jay West who was there to minister at a local church. I stated that I was and asked how he knew that. He went on to explain that his cousin attends that church and he had heard that I was coming in at my own expense to bless this smaller church on the El Paso and Juarez border.

He then told me that he was the assistant manager, that he was also a believer, and that he wanted to bless me for offering to bless this church. So he upgraded me to a full suite in a very quiet section of the hotel. This room had a kitchen, a living area, a king-sized bed, and a Jacuzzi bath tub that was literally six feet in length. He also reduced my regular room rate from around sixty-five dollars to a mere twenty-seven dollars for my entire stay.

What happened? I gave and sowed into a Hispanic brother in Omaha and three days later, a Hispanic brother sowed into my life in El Paso. This is the way the kingdom of God works and is the subject of our study in this chapter. We will learn that as we yield to God with our finances, He will in turn bring a yield back to us. I sowed around fifteen or twenty dollars, but I received a far greater value in return, probably closer to 200 dollars for the four nights I was in El Paso.

In Malachi 3:7–12 we read these words:

"Yet from the days of your fathers you have gone away from My ordinances and have not kept them. Return to Me, and I will return to you," says the LORD of hosts.

> "But you said, 'In what way shall we return?' Will a man rob God? Yet you have robbed Me!
>
> But you say, 'In what way have we robbed You?' In tithes and offerings. You are cursed with a curse, for you have robbed Me, even this whole nation. Bring all the tithes into the storehouse, that there may be food in My house, and try Me now in this," says the LORD of hosts, "If I will not open for you the windows of heaven and pour out for you such blessing that there will not be room enough to receive it. And I will rebuke the devourer for your sakes, so that he will not destroy the fruit of your ground, nor shall the vine fail to bear fruit for you in the field," says the LORD of hosts; "And all nations will call you blessed, for you will be a delightful land," says the LORD of hosts.

I am going to reveal some of this to you in a teaching form that makes some sense. The goal is to bring greater clarity with a deeper level of understanding that advances kingdom thought to then produce a harvest for you too. You may remember that in chapter eleven I wrote about Stephen's message in Acts 7, where in verse 51 he told the religious crowd that many in the congregation were resisting the Holy Spirit just like their fathers had done. I then compared that to King David's wife Michal, who also took on the characteristics of her father, King Saul. Here in Malachi 3:7 we see a similar scenario setting up.

> "Yet from the days of your fathers you have gone away from My ordinances and have not kept them. Return to Me, and I will return to you," says the LORD of hosts.
>
> "But you said, 'In what way shall we return?'"

God is problem-solving, not with blame, but with recognition that a particular issue is occurring that started with their fathers. This trend just seems to repeat itself over and over in the Bible. The problem is that because we are raised a certain way, we think that it must be the correct way. We want to believe that our parents were acting in our best interest and would not intentionally go against what the Lord had told them to do. God's solution to the problem is for the people to return to Him. The people don't understand because they have been doing what their fathers did. They don't think that they have moved away from God, so they question with the words, "In what ways shall we return?" It's a logical response because they honestly don't think that they have strayed away from God at all.

Before I address the rest of the passage, there is a trend today to do the very same thing. Many are convinced that tithing and giving offerings is old school, and this theology that has invaded the church that has sharp spiritual cancerous affects. That is a strong statement that I will clarify as we get into a deeper discussion of this passage, but opposing the command to tithe is a very dangerous position to take in today's society.

The people have just asked God how to return, and God's response to that is here in verse eight.

Will a man rob God? Yet you have robbed Me!

But you say, "In what way have we robbed You?" In tithes and offerings.

God's answer is that the "returning to Him" has to be in the area of tithes and offerings. The people still don't get it because they have been fooled into thinking that not giving to God in this manner is okay. In their logical minds, it does not make sense to them, so they ask another question about how they might be robbing God. They honestly don't understand that this tragic mistake may be costing them their very livelihood. It is imperative for them to understand that by not participating in tithes and offerings, they are indeed journeying away from God, and that movement away is actually robbing them of true friendship, kinship, and a presence-based relationship with the Lord. By not yielding to God in this area, it is creating a rift between them and God—a spiritual chasm, if you will, that is not easily bridged without the people returning to God with a correct attitude adjustment and application assessment.

I've heard it said that when you are not giving tithes and offerings, you are essentially driving a stolen car, watching a stolen television, and sleeping on a stolen bed. The word *tithe* literally means "a tenth," or the first ten percent of your income. I have personally been tithing since I was fifteen and don't plan to stop this side of heaven. Years ago, I heard Jack Taylor say that some people will ask if they should tithe on the "gross" income or the "net" income. Jack went on to say, "If you have to ask, it's gross."

I want to center on verses 10 and 11 for a little while.

> Bring all the tithes into the storehouse, that there may be food in My house, and try Me now in this," says the LORD of hosts, "If I will not open for you the windows of heaven and pour out for you such blessing that there will not be room enough to receive it. And I will rebuke the devourer for your sakes, so that he will not destroy the fruit of your ground, nor shall the vine fail to bear fruit for you in the field," says the LORD of hosts.

When I was a senior pastor I would challenge the people to bring their tithes, not just send it in. I know there is a comfort and an ease from sometimes sending in your tithe, but the offering is a time of worship whenever you meet corporately, and when you send it in, you lose that aspect of worship. Often, I would also encourage people not to split their tithe by giving to the local church and then to another ministry. Offerings are for those purposes of helping others and other ministries.

I heard Myles Munroe teach on this once in a message in which he said that the tithe is like paying taxes to your local community. Tithes are for the maintenance of your area, but offerings are for exploration. I like those definitions, as they help bring clarity. I knew people who would send part of their tithe to a national ministry. I challenged them on these types of "experiments" that really don't quite line up with the Word of God. Also, when I discovered repeat offenders of this principle, I would encourage them to call that national ministry when they had a problem in the middle of the night or went into the hospital or even had some marriage problems. The reason is because by sending the tithe to the national ministry, that ministry has now become their pastor.

I take this seriously to this day, and when I hear others say that they are going to send me a part of their tithe, I will discourage them from doing that. Obviously, I don't want to lose their contribution, but even more important than that, I want them to be responding to God's command in an effective, biblical way.

Notice too that verse 10 says that there will be food in my house. I hear people say that they just don't get fed at their local church anymore. They might simply state that the feeding isn't what it used to be when they first started attending. Frequently, my first question upon hearing this is to ask if they are still tithing. Often, the answer is no, they have dropped it down considerably or stopped altogether. This is KEY! You must understand that when you tithe, God does something supernaturally with the spiritual food you are receiving. It genuinely tastes good, and you enjoy spiritual meat at your local church. It really is an amazing process.

Matthew 6:21 says, "Where your treasure is, there your heart will be also." Sometimes as I hear of friends looking for a new church, there is a tendency to attend one church one week and another the next week, and so on, just shopping and hopping from one place to another. First of all, any church can have a really good day or a really bad day on the one you select to attend, so I challenge folks who are looking for a new church to attend that church for a whole month before moving on to another church. Second, according to Matthew 6:21, I encourage them to tithe and give offerings at this local church for that whole month too. If their heart follows the giving, then that is probably a good place for them to land and connect. But if not, then move on and try another place for a month. This process has proven helpful, faithful, and true to many people searching for a new church fellowship.

In Malachi 3:10, God promises to open up the windows of heaven and pour out a blessing. This is a tremendous promise and revolves around the word *yield* once again. The word *blessing* comes from the Latin word "benediction." Let's dissect benediction for just a moment. *Bene* literally means "good," and *diction* means "word." That is where we get our English word *dictionary*. I am sure you see the picture. When God says that He is going to pour out a blessing, some of the ways that He may choose to do that are by releasing a good word in your life that will enable you to be creative and innovative, while enjoying the favor of God in any area that He wants to bless in your life that can cause you to make more money or acquire things that money can't buy.

Giving the tithes and offerings really isn't so much about giving something to God, but rather about trusting Him with something you already have so that you can receive His blessing or benediction (a good word in your life). Sometimes, He does rain down money out of heaven, but that is not the norm. Rather, He rains down ideas that help you to make more money. For instance, we heard of a believer in another state who created a way to recycle Styrofoam, and a large, well-known company purchased the patent to this idea for millions of dollars.

On the flip side, I want to share a quick story of friends of ours in Dallas who had a $200 bill to pay on Monday. These folks were tithers, and they had been praying for God to provide it for them. The man of the house mowed his lawn late Saturday evening, and when he awoke on Sunday morning, he went out to retrieve the newspaper. Right in the middle of this newly-mown lawn were two 100 dollar bills. Now, that is amazing, and God can and does bless like that from time to time too. After all, it's His deal and His promise to fulfill, so He can do it like He pleases.

In verse eleven, God says He will rebuke the devourer for us and on our behalf. Shoot, I would continue to tithe for this reason alone. The enemy tries to come into our lives in so many subtle and hidden ways, to get and gain a foothold that he can use at another and more convenient time. Let me illustrate with this story. Years ago, just after Diane and I got married, we had given away most of our furniture to a missionary couple, and we were left without any living room tables of any kind. There was a new company that was producing a kind of rustic-looking furniture that had an Amish flavor to it. It was called Cargo Furniture. We liked it and started collecting it, initially with the living room pieces.

A couple of years later, we had increased our Cargo Furniture acquisitions and were now ready to buy his and hers dressers for our bedroom. So I drove off to the local franchise that was close to us at the time in Houston. Somehow, I engaged the manager in a conversation about God and discovered that this gentleman was a believer. We had a nice visit about the Lord prior to actually talking about the two dressers that we wanted to purchase that day.

As we were about to make the deal and sign on the dotted line for these two pieces to be delivered, this man then offered me a small end table for free as a token gift for buying the other two pieces. I asked him if this was a promotion and he said, no, they just do this all the time to encourage repeat customers. I asked him how the parent company could make such an ongoing promotion, and he stated that they knew nothing about it. He simply would tell the parent company that some pieces came broken and then would give them away to good paying customers like myself.

At this point in the transaction, my credit card was in my hand, and I was just about to slide it across the counter to hand it to him for the purchase. But suddenly, I pulled it back while asking if this was dishonest. His response startled me when he said, "Managers and real leaders do it all the time." I then told him I can't participate in this unjust and deceptive practice, especially after we had just engaged in twenty minutes of conversation about God and sharing Bible passages and testimonies.

He said it was no big deal and that people do it all the time, and I countered by saying, "Well, people may do it all the time, but this person is not going to participate in it at all. I am not going to purchase these dressers at your store." He then told me I was a fool and I would never find such a bargain plus a free piece of furniture with it. I said, "That may be, but I will at least be walking in godly integrity." Then, I promptly left the store.

Two days later in Houston, a large, locally owned furniture store called Fingers Furniture came out with a brand new line of rustic furniture called Barn Door. I went to check it out with Diane, and we ended up buying our two new dressers that matched perfectly with our other furniture. We actually purchased these dressers for less than what we would have paid for the two at Cargo. I know that God gave us a "bene-diction." I believe that God rebuked the devourer on our behalf and that we were blessed by God that day for walking in godly integrity and not allowing the enemy access into that part of our lives. The net result is that we have those two pieces to this day, and they have weathered better and survived multiple moves and locations better than any of the other furniture that we have.

I don't think I was foolish at all in turning down the extra table offer. Instead, it would have really been foolish to go against what I know to be biblically true. By following God's advice in Malachi, I believe I received a yield back in my life that was substantially more than what I yielded in the first place. I did not list it in the original passage from Malachi, but the first offering in Malachi 3 is in verse 3, which is an offering in righteousness. God is far more interested in our righteousness than He is in our trust with our stuff. If we respond righteously and give an offering in righteousness, I am convinced that all other offerings and giving experiences will dovetail off that and platform dive into greater depths with God that will ultimately produce more blessings and benediction moments in our lives.

The meat of verse eleven is about to be revealed, so I am writing the verse once again for you to read.

> And I will rebuke the devourer for your sakes, so that he will not destroy the fruit of your ground, nor shall the vine fail to bear fruit for you in the field," says the LORD of hosts.

God does not want the enemy to destroy the fruit of our ground. Why do you think this is important? After all, the majority of the population doesn't farm anymore, so these verses can't just pertain to farmers, can they? Of course not. There is a message hidden here waiting to be revealed and applied.

What happens if the fruit is destroyed? First of all, the actual eating of that harvest has now been eliminated and could cause you and me a hardship because of the lack of food. Every farmer knows that the harvest is measured in the number of bushels or weight of the harvest itself. But there is another critical ingredient that must not be overlooked. Every good farmer knows that not only is the produce itself important, but within that produce is more seed to plant next year. If the fruit is destroyed, so is the seed, and thus ends all future harvest seasons too.

Seed is very, very important to all farmers. If they can't get seed from their crops, then they have to purchase it elsewhere. In the natural, that may be okay; but in the spiritual, if you have to secure your seed from another source other than God, it is going to be seed that is far inferior to anything God can provide. When people rob God by driving stolen cars and watching stolen televisions, what often happens is that they are so in debt to these purchases. Then, when a great opportunity comes along to sow into a ministry, give to the poor, or bless another minister, they shamefully don't give because they have no seed to sow because it is all wrapped up in monthly payments at their local bank or some credit card agency. The fruit has been destroyed, and it lies rotting on the ground. The seed that could have been sown to produce a greater harvest with even more seed for future plantings is now lying wasted and barren on the ground. It is useless and has lost all ability to receive a benediction.

Most people who know me know my heart, and my heart is to give and to bless often, wherever God may open the door for me to do that. The reality is that more and more stuff keeps coming back to us. Now, some might say that I give to get, and that is only two-thirds correct. For you see, I give to get so I can give again and keep on blessing, helping, and assisting, while honoring God with my money and my stuff. Over the years, we have given away furniture, refrigerators, cars, land, and various sums of money, and we have always seen it return in a great heavenly yield from our Father in heaven. You have already read many such stories in this book.

Before I get to the last few points of this study time, let me share yet another story. I was in the Chicago area ministering at a local church. The church was fan-shaped, and there were probably close to 300 people in this packed little church in Geneva, Illinois. During the worship, as I was sitting way over on the right side of the building, God instructed me to go over to the far left side of the building where He would lead me to a couple who were unemployed with two smaller children at home. As I walked to the other side, I was asking the Lord to show me the exact couple so that I would not interrupt anyone's time of worship that was going on by trying to find out which couple it was.

Sure enough, God led me to the right couple, and I explained that God had sent me over to find them and to pray for them. After my prayer, I knew that God also wanted me to give them something financially, so I sat down to pray about this. Every time I travel, I take a blank check with me in my wallet because God often prompts me to help people when traveling. That night would be no different.

As I was praying, I asked God what I should give, and He simply responded, "You decide." I did not like this answer, as I had no idea what their need was, nor would I be able to figure it out without talking to them. I did not want to embarrass them. So, I asked God if He would just give me an amount, and I would gladly write out a check for that amount. But once again, God told me to decide.

This was very unusual because in the past God had always given me an amount. I sat there thinking about a family of four, their financial needs, and how much it might cost to feed a family of four for a week or a month. Then I decided that I would write out a check for $250. I had already secured their names, stating I would pray for them, so I wrote out the check and delivered

Study Time: Part 5

it to them, to which I received multiple hugs and astonished looks of gratitude. I shared the experience with no one.

One of the things that has marked this ministry is that I don't have a local church signup list for people to subscribe to a monthly newsletter or appeal letter. When money comes to us in the mail, it is generally a surprise. When I got home that week from Chicago, I would receive three such surprises.

I arrived home on Monday, and on Friday as I went to the mailbox to retrieve the mail, I noticed that the first letter on top was from an Omaha megachurch called Trinity Church, now called Lifegate. I had never ministered at this church, so I was hopeful that it might be an invitation. When I opened the envelope, inside was a note from the associate pastor representing the senior pastor, with a message that went something like this: "Jay, we know that you travel to many small churches and often bless so many others, and while we have not had you in to minister here yet, we want to bless you with this love offering to help your ministry." Inside was a folded check for $2500. I just gave away $250 to total strangers, and here six days later I was receiving a check for ten times that amount! By the way, I have now ministered at this church several times. But the story does not stop there.

The next envelope was from still another large church in town called King of Kings Lutheran Church. This one was expected, though, as I was teaching a class on Tuesday evenings at this church. They would take a love offering for me at each class, and then the money would be counted the next day, with a check cut and mailed to me. I generally would receive it by Fridays. Inside, I expected to find a check for the love offering of $247, but instead I found a check for $1247. I concluded that someone had made a mistake, so I went in the house to call them up and let them know.

The financial treasurer was grateful for my call and told me just to hang on to the check for a few minutes while they decided if they wanted me to send it back or just shred it at home, and they would mail me a corrected check. Sure enough, in a very short amount of time, they called back but with surprising news. The offering part of $247 from the class was correct, but on Wednesday morning of that week, someone had come in and anonymously donated an additional $1000.

There I was six days later with an additional $3500 in my possession after giving that money away in Chicago, but can you believe there is a little bit more? I then opened up an envelope from a church in Idaho where I had previously ministered. I did not know what to expect, although I had been in communication with them. They had previously had me in to minister and really enjoyed it, so they invited me back, but had fallen on some difficult financial times and told me that they could not afford to pay for my airfare. I had prayed and felt I should go anyway, offering to pay for my ticket as a blessing to them. I had already purchased the ticket a few weeks prior. This was the church in Sandpoint where God had me pray the fifteen-inch snowstorm away.

As I opened the envelope, and read their card, I was truly surprised when they wrote that they too had received some financial provision and that they could now afford to pay for my airfare. As I recall, they sent me slightly more than the actual cost of the flight at around $500. Here I was with a yield totaling $4000 or so from my "seed planting" in Chicago of $250. Not a bad deal, if you ask me. I believe that the next part of verse 11 was also being yielded back to me where it says that neither shall your vine fail to bear fruit for you. Let me explain.

In Song of Solomon 2:15 there is a warning to beware of the little foxes that can spoil the vine. This is a critical verse that helps us understand the last line of Malachi 3:11. As you may know, many wild animals get their moisture from eating leaves and fruit from plants. The adult animals can reach up and easily eat the leaves or fruit on a vine or tree. But smaller animals that have not developed can't reach up that high, but they are still thirsty too. Thus, they will often nibble at the base of the plant where the vine or stalk disappears into the ground. Many times when they do this, they chew right through the primary source for the nutrients and water to get to the rest of the plant, thus killing the whole plant. It is a reality of the animal kingdom.

God's promise is that our vine will not fail to yield fruit to us for those who tithe and give offerings. There may be droughts and storms, but His provision remains faithful even in the darkest and worst of times. His provision has been my family's theophany as we have trusted in the theology of giving, sowing, and reaping through tithing with offerings. God has never let us down, and we have always received back more than we gave in the first place. I can't think of one exception. Now, not every response of reaping has been as fast as others. A number of years ago we planted a garden consisting of radishes, onions, squash, carrots, watermelon, and other garden foods. Radishes were up in 14 days, but watermelons took all summer, even though they were planted on the same day.

When we give, we don't always see the return the next day, but we do see it when we need it. We live in a position of sowing every week into someone or some ministry because we believe Isaiah 32:8, which says that a generous man shall devise generous things and by generosity he shall stand. I love this verse and frequently look for ways to be generous. I challenge you to do the same.

Every once in a while, Pastor Jim Hart at our church will quote the Bible where it says God loves a cheerful giver (2 Cor. 9:7). Then he kiddingly adds in, "But He will take it from a grouch!" While that is true, I prefer to have a smile on my face when I give and to give cheerfully, knowing that I am helping to expand and advance the kingdom of God. I want to experience joy in my life, so I give joyfully, full of anticipation and wonder, without doubt, sadness, or despair. God is the source of my life, and I want my giving to reflect that provision and my walk with Jesus as being a friendly one, not one based out of compulsion or hype or some sort of personal agenda.

If Jesus is the agenda, then my giving flows out of my relationship with Jesus and is never a chore or a religious law or even some sort of churchy thing that I do. Rather, it is a life-sustaining option that God freely gives to me because I have simply yielded to His plan.

Regarding the radishes and watermelons above, I could give you many examples when the reaping that we were anticipating came just in time, not early or late. My calendar anticipation may not line up with what God wants to do, but His timing is always accurate, and I have no complaints. It's a powerful testimony to see and experience this on a consistent basis. As verse 12 indicates, over the years, many others have affirmed that we are indeed blessed. The benedictions arrived, and we did receive what He promised. It was not always easy, but it has always been worth it, and I believe that it will be worth it for you too.

Journey

Now, what do you do? If you are already tithing and giving offerings, you are already enjoying this journey and you personally can attest to God's blessing and faithfulness in your life. But if this is new to you, then you have to consider carefully your next steps.

Maybe you are in a church that no longer teaches that the message in Malachi chapter three is relevant for today. Or maybe you have just never tithed, even though you have heard it taught many times in the past. Whatever the reason, I encourage you to pause and reflect over some of what you just read and ask God if He would have you begin to increase your giving. Let Him be your guide. You have read my illustrations and teaching, but you must hear from the Lord too.

For me, 10% is just a starting point. Most years as a family, we give well beyond that. We don't look at the tithe as the end of our giving but only the beginning. We have a friend in the San Antonio area who lives on 10% of his income and gives 90% away. We have heard the testimony of a man originally from China now living in Los Angeles who keeps giving 100% of his income away, while God just provides everything he needs. I'm not there yet. But I am growing into increased giving each year, and we keep seeing our yield being increased back to us too. We don't give to get, but it is a reality of the kingdom. We do give to get and then give even more again. This kingdom principle has proven to be reliable over and over.

I really can't tell you how to take the next step of your journey regarding this subject. And I would not want to. I want you to experience God and see Him move in your life as you respond to His promptings. But I do want to hear your testimonies, so please write to me and share them on my blog at **www.anointed2go.com**. I would be delighted to hear from you. I just know God is going to do something amazing and incredible through you as you yield even more in this area.

Remember, God doesn't need your money, but you need His blessing. Wouldn't it be great to get a "bene diction," or a good word, from God today that truly will enable you to walk in faith like you never have before, demonstrating the faithfulness and provision of heaven on earth where you live right now?

Will you be that generous person that Isaiah 32:8 speaks about? Will you yield to His plan? What will you do now? I urge you to begin to position yourself to respond to what God is asking you to do, with great anticipation and joy, without any doubt, believing that this plan is His plan. As you work the Word of God, the Word of God will work for you.

Chapter Sixteen

Completing the Challenge Course

My paraphrased version of Galatians 5:7 asks the question, "You used to run well; who has hindered you from obeying the truth?" The Message Bible puts it this way: "You were running superbly! Who cut in on you, deflecting you from the true course of obedience? This detour doesn't come from the One who called you into the race in the first place." It's been said that life's detours are often God's interstate highways. Someone else once said that obstacles are those things that we see when we take our eyes off of the goal. As I wrote in Chapter 4, we should glance at the problem and gaze at God.[17] That is good advice.

Willing to Yield has been a collection of stories and teachings written with the intended purpose of disclosing to you how yielding to God can then bring a yield from God back to you. But we must understand that the enemy is at work too, trying to distract us and stop us from experiencing God in this way. The enemy's intent is to kill, rob, and destroy any work of God in our lives. To be honest, he is just following his self-imposed job description. If he can rob even some of our faith from us and get us to doubt, then we become substantially less capable, with less oomph and less ability truly to make a difference. It's kind of like losing a couple of spark plugs from your car or tractor. The engine can still function, and you will have some power, but it will be a rough and slow ride for sure.

I recently posted a note on Facebook that originated with me. To preface this quote, I must state that I am a church growth advocate and love to see the kingdom expand and grow. I am certainly open to new ideas and innovative approaches, but I want to emphasize that growth *for* the kingdom without growth *in* the kingdom is not valid. Jesus said on several occasions and in various ways that the kingdom of heaven is at hand. Whenever I read one of those passages, I ask people to hold out their hands. I generally ask them what their hands are connected to, and they respond to their arms or their bodies. I then ask them to consider how close the kingdom of God always is. It literally is within arm's distance and close at hand. Since it is so close, the kingdom should be having a great impact on our own lives, and we should be experiencing measured growth.

Romans 12:3 states that faith comes in a measure. In other places in the Bible, we are told that we are progressing from faith to faith. In other words, faith is given in a measure, and God expects that measure to grow and increase. On the other hand, John 3:34 states that the Holy Spirit is given without measure, so God backs up our measured and growing faith with unmeasured power. It's a winning combination for us as believers.

Jesus said in John 5:19 that He only did what He saw the Father doing, and that is our mandate as well. We can read all the church growth books and devour and implement every method and example that other churches and ministries have found to be successful. Yet, if we yield to their definitions and methods that they were successful at, rather than doing what Jesus is calling you to do, we will miss the kingdom entirely because our focus is off. If Jesus says to do what the church growth manual book says to do, then do that for sure. But be open to the possibility that for your unique situation and your church environment, God may direct you to do something radically different that may even require more faith. In the end, when His results are met, God will get the glory and you will reap the benefits.

Second Corinthians 5:9 states, "Therefore, we make it our aim, whether present or absent, to be well pleasing to Him." Simply put, if you were to look down the sight of a gun, regardless of the type of gun, if the sight is off, you will probably miss the intended target. If the object you are shooting at is close at hand and large enough, you might hit the target. But the further the bullet or pellet travels away from the gun, the larger the difference will be from where the projectile hits and what the target actually is.

Several years ago, we had a robin that would sit on an evergreen branch and then fly directly into our living room window over and over, hundreds of times a day. I guess he thought that his reflection was an enemy bird, so he was trying to attack the bird. Initially, it was comical, but after a week of this constant pounding, beginning as early as 5:30 a.m. and lasting until almost totally dark at 9:00 p.m., it was becoming a huge nuisance. We tried a variety of things to scare off the bird such as hanging wind chimes, positioning fake owls, and even placing a sheet over the window, all to no avail. There are a number of videos on YouTube that show this very thing happening to other frustrated home owners too.

A friend of mine loaned us a BB gun, so I began to wait for the bird and would carefully aim, only to have the BB miss the bird wide to the left each time. I soon realized that the sight was off quite a bit, so I had to overshoot to the right, but I still repeatedly missed the bird, simply because my aim was not precise and where it should be.

When our aim is not centered on Jesus, but rather on some method, although appearing very successful in one location or at a particular church, it may not be meant for your church to try. I frequently tell pastors that just because the church down the street has a soup kitchen doesn't mean your church is supposed to have one. Or just because a church near you has a bus ministry picking up children and bringing them to their church doesn't mean your church is supposed to do the same. We need to discover what the Lord is doing at our location and then proceed with His plans, not someone else's plans. There are good strategies, and then there are God's plans. While slightly out of context, Jeremiah 29:11 offers great sound advice that God's plans and thoughts are for peace and to give us a future and a hope. Anyone who has been around church long enough knows what that lack of peace feels like when launching a plan that did not have God's stamp of approval on it.

With that in mind, here is what I wrote: "If the purpose-driven church is not driven by the power of the Holy Spirit and purposed in following Jesus, then maybe that church is driving the wrong direction with the wrong purpose." Our aim is radically off course if our plans don't include a steady offering of the power of the Holy Spirit and the opportunity for people to meet and fall in love with Jesus.

An offensive runner or end on a football team makes it his aim to cross the goal line and score while carrying the ball. That is how touchdowns are scored. If a tight end runs across the goal line and the quarterback beans him on the back of his helmet with a pass, causing the ball to deflect somewhere off the field, that is not considered a touchdown because, while the aim of the quarterback may have been accurate, the aim of the game had been defeated.

A baseball player makes it his aim to touch all of the bases with one foot after hitting the ball. If he misses one and the umpire sees it, he can be called out. A defensive player in baseball can get the opposing player out by touching the correct base or the player while holding onto the ball. However, he must follow the rules of the game. He can't simply throw the ball at the player who is running from first to second and hit him in the shins, the shoulder, or the head in order to get him out. While his aim may be good enough to accomplish that, he will most likely be thrown out of the game for not making it his aim to follow the rules of the game.

I used to love to play tennis and still enjoy watching it. When serving, you have to serve within the correct square on the opponent's side in order for the serve to be legal. If the serve hits the net first and then the ball still goes in the correct place, the serve is repeated as the net has caused the angle and speed of the ball to be altered, thus disrupting the aim of the game itself. This distraction could also cause an injury to the receiving player as well. This is called a "let." Outside of this net-hitting let, you normally only get two service tries to get that tennis ball into the right square. There are exceptions, but if you miss in a normal way, you can't say the wind or the sun or someone in the crowd bothered you and you want another try. You have simply missed the aim of the game and must proceed according to the rules.

Most amateur players usually dink the second serve in so as not to lose a point on a serve. I always hit the second serve just as hard as the first. I knew my tennis skills, and my serve was pretty good, so the odds of the second serve going in were good. It always took my opponent by surprise. Besides, a good tennis player overcomes all obstacles. And a believer in Jesus can overcome all obstacles with the power of the Holy Spirit, the Word of God, and Jesus. What a superior combination!

We used to have a Snoopy poster with Snoopy standing on a tennis court, holding a racket. The caption on the poster read, "It doesn't matter if you win or lose, until you lose." Paul wrote to Timothy and said to fight the good fight of faith. I have often stated that a good fight is one that you win. You can be lying in the dust and bleeding, but if you won, it was still a good fight. God expects us to win if we march to His strategies and use His plans, but when we go off on our own, that is a dangerous position in which to be.

My dad taught me how to play tennis. He was a Physical Education major with a master's degree after playing pro football for the Rams and prior to that as quarterback for the Pittsburgh Panthers. He also played in the Cotton Bowl in Dallas. My dad's name was Walt, and if he served a double fault, I would always say, "That's a fault, Walt." He would smile and generally win the next point. My dad, like any other dad, also had other faults, but he played to win, regardless of whether it was football, tennis, golf, cribbage, or chess. He had a winning attitude that was attractive to others. It was often said that my dad could talk to anyone, and I believe I have that trait too.

I wear Dad's college football ring to this day. That is my way of aiming to stay connected to him, even though he has been gone now since 1984. It was a joy to introduce him to Jesus back in the late-'70s, which was several years prior to him being attacked with a brain tumor that ultimately took his life. My dad was on the winning team even in death. All those who put their trust in Jesus as their Savior and Lord are also on the winning team.

Dad had a sign made that hung at the entrance of our long circular California driveway—and by long, I mean long. We could probably park eighteen cars in our driveway at one time. The sign simply stated: W. J. West and Team. From time to time, Dad would remind us that we were all on the same team. So today, if you are a believer in Jesus, regardless of your denominational persuasion or theological beliefs, I want to remind you that we are all on the same team. That sign still hangs at the entrance of our home today right under another similar sign for our family. If you are interested, you can find the picture of Walter James West and some football stats on Wikipedia.

Regarding a biblical sign that God asks us to hang up and display, read these words from Deuteronomy 6:6–9:

> And these words which I command you today shall be in your heart. You shall teach them diligently to your children, and shall talk of them when you sit in your house, when you walk by the way, when you lie down, and when you rise up. You shall bind them as a sign on your hand, and they shall be as frontlets between your eyes. You shall write them on the doorposts of your house and on your gates.

I have another football friend that I want to tell you about. His name is Sid Smith. Sid was an All American Tackle at the University of Southern California for four years. Then he went on to play pro football as a center for the Kansas City Chiefs and finally retired after playing for the Houston Oilers, which is where I met him down in Texas.

Sid got saved early on as a child and lived for Jesus all of his life. When Sid left pro football, he became a very good and well sought-after home builder for ten years in the Houston area. However, he made some mistakes, and as he says, he kind of became wrapped up in himself when he took his aim off Jesus and had to declare bankruptcy. That hindrance made it difficult for him to run well in that realm.

Later, he went into the insurance business and kept his eyes on the Lord. His State Farm agency grew into the top ten percent of all of the State Farm agencies in the state of Texas. Sid is married and has two wonderful children with his lovely and anointed wife Cynthia.

At one point while working for State Farm, Sid decided to open another office further out into the suburbs. Prior to doing that, he contacted all of the other agents in that particular geographical area, told them of his intentions, and offered to stay away from any area that any of those other agents already considered their turf. This is generally unheard of in the dog-eat-dog business sector. Many business leaders would not even consider another person while trying to grow their own businesses, but Sid had learned his lesson and was now yielding more completely to God. Psalm 112:5 says that a good man deals graciously and lends and that he will guide his affairs with discretion. Sid is a good man, and he does guide his business affairs with discretion.

One of Sid's major clients was Shipley Donuts, which is a huge donut chain throughout the state of Texas and other states as well, with a total of 250 franchises. Sid insured the whole company. Or is that the hole company? (Smile)

Anyway, years later Sid decided he wanted to open his own Shipley Donuts franchise too, so while still operating his insurance company. He opened this donut franchise just a couple of blocks away in a new shopping center that had multiple stores built; however, all of them stood empty, except for this one donut store. Would you believe that Sid's one donut store outsold all of the other Shipley stores for the first year? What happened? How is that possible? Think of it: The only reason you would ever pull into

Completing the Challenge Course

this shopping area was to turn around or to buy donuts. This has to be the favor of God. There is no other explanation. Sid made it his aim to be well pleasing to God. He yielded his life to the Lord, and God obviously brought a great yield back to him. I can't say enough about this godly man, which is why I co-dedicated this book to him.

At one point, Sid gained some weight. He knew since I was from Southern California that one of the college teams I enjoy following is USC, so he gave me a jersey that no longer fit him. I wore it with pride, mostly because it was Sid's jersey. But later Sid lost that weight, and I felt led to give it back to him. It seemed like the right thing to do. This book is dedicated in part to my friend Sid Smith because he dedicated his life to Jesus.

Several years ago I found a lady's gold ring in a love offering that was given to me at a church where I was ministering. I had the ring appraised for $400, and I tried to discover who had given me such a nice ring. I finally found out who gave it and learned that the lady's husband was not happy that she had given the ring away. He was godly and understood her reasons, but he was also disappointed, as that was the first ring he gave her prior to their marriage. Even though we could have certainly used the $400 at that time in our lives, I chose to give the ring back. It seemed like the right thing to do. Jesus is in the business of restoring lost things to people who trust in Him, so I knew I had the right attitude in this as well. As a result, God later yielded something special back to me from that same congregation and the pastor who was there at the time. Here is that account.

In 2006, we were looking for a second car, as we had been a one-car family for eleven years. With Jason entering high school, we felt that we needed a second car. It is not easy for me, being tall, to find a car. Many cars may look good but will lack head room or leg or knee room, etc., so my choices are limited. I had discovered a used automobile that I could fit into that also got good gas mileage. However, my trip to this church was the next day, so I decided not to make a quick decision and work on it after I returned.

I drove four hours over to Ottumwa, Iowa, where I was to minister. The pastor, whose name was Dave, heard my story about looking for a car and encouraged me to look at an ad in their local paper. He told me it was for a new Monte Carlo that this guy who worked for Dollar General had won because of his performance for the company. I resisted looking at the ad, as

I was not looking for a new Monte Carlo. But eventually, after considerable coaxing from the pastor, I read the ad and made an appointment to go view the car.

I was surprised that it drove so well and that I fit in it nicely too. Plus the man was selling this brand new car with only a couple of hundred miles on it for $5000 below retail. After a little negotiation, he lowered it another $2000. So a decision to purchase this car was made in just fifteen minutes. The normal way that I buy a car is that I go find one, then test drive it, then come home and pray about it, then repeat the process the next day, coming home and praying again and normally going back the third time to discover that the car has sold. Making a decision in fifteen minutes or so was new to me.

My mother had just passed away a few months prior to this, and we had an inheritance from her that we had planned to use on this car purchase. I called Diane at home and asked her to transfer the necessary money, and we got a brand new car with a three-year bumper-to-bumper warranty for the same price that I was going to pay for a used car with around 75,000 miles on it and no warranty. Isn't God good? I believe we were receiving an extended yield like an extended warranty for some of the cars we had previously given away.

But I was four hours from home with two cars and only one driver. Pastor Dave was so gracious that he offered to drive one car, and I drove one car, and his wife drove their car four hours to our place and then four hours home, just to bless us. I know I got much greater than the value of that ring back on that one for sure. Do you see how yielding works?

By the way, thanks Mom for storing up an inheritance for your sons too. That was an incredible blessing that meant so much. My mom, Barbara West, worked for many years at Bank of America to help leave us something after she passed. When your parents work to bless you, you know you have good parents. I still have the car to this day, and it's Nebraska Red. Go Cornhuskers! Okay, get over it. We follow four teams. USC because I am from Southern California, Wisconsin because Diane is from Wisconsin, University of Texas because Jason was born in Texas, and Nebraska because this is where we have lived since 2000, not counting our college years here too. Lately, I have been hearing some amazing and incredibly cool things about Coach Bob Stoops from Oklahoma who is the brother-in-law of some good friends of ours. So I think I am adding a fifth team into the mix. Surely, one of them can win the national championship.

As I was writing this section, it occurred to me that there is another cool connection to this particular car. Back in the early-'70s when I was in high school, my parents bought one of the newer Monte Carlos of that day. It was a nice forest green color with a white landau roof and had amazingly comfortable seats with all of the bells and whistles included. It was primarily my mother's car to drive, although we did take family trips in it. My dad had a baby blue 1967 Mustang. Obviously, I enjoyed driving both cars, but the remembrance and connection of that Monte Carlo to the one we have now is special as I remember my mom and my dad and the influence they had on my life.

Mom insisted that my older brother Jim and I go to church, VBS, and other activities. Then it was on to youth group, which later faltered when our exceptional youth leader named Lynn moved away to another city. Lynn was a great guy who loved the Lord and yielded his life to God. He is still a friend of mine to this day. But the influence of my mom taking me to church activities has impacted my life to this day. It was and is a blessing which has yielded much fruit over the years.

When we make it our aim to be pleasing to God, Proverbs 16:7 says that God compels even our enemies to be at peace with us. Wow, this is a tremendous promise! It is very similar to that promise you learned about in the last chapter from Malachi 3 in which God rebukes the devourer on our behalf. Nothing beats serving Jesus with all of your heart, mind, soul, and life.

I launched this chapter with Galatians 5:7, and I want to return to that verse at this juncture. Running well with a firm stride can be hampered if we aren't careful. Our son Jason has recorded and released a worship album called *Running Free*. The first song, "Run with Freedom,"[18] has the following words that are so applicable to this chapter that I am listing them here for you to read:

> My feet are tired; I've run this race.
> I've trusted You; You've set the pace.
> I've given it all that I have to give.
> The finish line is now in sight,
> So I press on with all my might,

Living in the freedom that You give.

And I'll run into Your courts where I belong.
And I'll run into Your presence where I am strong.

I will run with freedom! I will dance with freedom!
I will jump with freedom in Your love!

The day is done; the price is paid.
The battle's won; I'll not be swayed.
I'm living in the promise of God's love.
The cause of Christ has set me free,
So now I live in victory.
The curse of sin is broken; death is done!

I'm turning ahead. I'm laying aside all my pride
And everything else that hinders the length of the stride,
Pressing on toward the goal of the heavenly prize.

We must pay attention to at least two things that the enemy loves to use to get us off track. Those two things are regret and anxiety. Regret almost always deals with the past, and anxiety usually deals with the future. We all have done, seen, and heard things that we wish we hadn't experienced, but if we give them to Jesus and cast those cares upon Him, He handles them and takes them away because He does care for us.

Several years ago, I was asked to pray for a medical massage therapist who was suffering with Carpal Tunnel Syndrome. This disease is painful enough, but as you can imagine, if you are using your hands to massage others, it had to be extremely difficult, if not excruciating. A local pastor friend asked me to pray for her. I agreed to meet with both of them, and we began to pray. While praying, I had a vision of a lady playing Frisbee in a park, and Jesus was there watching the game. Jesus spoke to the lady and asked her to toss Him a Frisbee too, stating that the Frisbee would represent her cares, so she began to do that, one Frisbee after another. But Jesus would never toss the Frisbees back.

I asked this massage therapist to begin to do that in her mind and to envision Jesus catching all of her Frisbees and cares but not returning them.

Finally, when she sensed she was finished, I encouraged her to see Jesus sitting on a park bench with his arm around her shoulder, smiling, laughing, and enjoying her company. At this point, I then prayed for her healing from the Carpal Tunnel Syndrome. All of her pain left her hands and wrists, and she was totally well. Jesus supernaturally healed this lady by massaging out her physical pain simply by having her toss Him all of her emotional pain too. Again, when our ways please the Lord, He makes even our enemies to be at peace with us.

Initially, my vision seemed weird to me because I don't normally act or flow that way under the power of the Holy Spirit, but I am glad I yielded to what God was doing and wanted to do. I've learned that the methods are only as good as the Master of the methods. If the method comes from Jesus, then since He is the Master, I am okay with flowing with that method. But if it has human interference and can only work if you do it a certain way prescribed by people, then I quickly shy away from it. Jesus prayed for blind people in the Bible six different ways, and one of them twice. Therefore, I don't pray for all sick people the same way, but I simply ask the Lord how I should proceed.

God says in Psalm 32:8, "I will instruct you and teach you in the way you should go; I will guide you with my eye." We need to have close eye-to-eye contact with the Lord. In Luke chapter four, after that beautiful narrative when Jesus read from Isaiah about the anointing being upon Him, He then closed the book and sat down. At this point, the eyes of all those in the synagogue were fixed upon Him. Everyone in the whole building had eye-to-eye contact with Jesus. That's what our priority has to be too. Can you see Him looking at you now?

I remember ministering at an Open Bible church in Des Moines. We prayed for a lady whose eyesight was so bad that she could only see the big "E" on the eye chart in a fuzzy way. After ten minutes of praying, she could read font size fourteen in someone's Bible. A similar thing happened at a local Hispanic church where I was invited to minister, in that another lady's eyes were blurry. Suddenly, she could see clearly, and to prove it, she stood up and started reading the Bible while everyone was cheering. Our spiritual eyes need improvement too, and looking back with regret can really ruin those spiritual eyes. In the process, our image of Jesus gets blurred, and we look at alternative things instead of God.

Willing to Yield

Regret is such a killer. It holds people motionless and keeps them bound up from moving into the future with the Lord because of past failures, sins, bad habits, and mistakes. Jesus has paid the price for our past and has redeemed us from the curse of every one of those past sins. The devil would love to utilize the curse of those sins to tie us up and prevent us from accessing God's kingdom in our lives.

The Bible tells us that our sins are removed as far as the East is from the West. We need to believe God when He says this because East and West never meet. We need to appropriate forgiveness and walk in freedom with Jesus. The Bible says whom the Son sets free is free indeed (John 8:36).

Joyce Meyer has effectively taught Galatians 5:7 with an illustrated sermon. I have copied her a few times, adding in some other options. Basically, Joyce ties up someone's hands, which demonstrates that person is still holding on to regret. Then someone is appointed to play the part of God, who goes around greeting others. Since we are supposed to do what we see the Father doing, that person whose hands are tied then tries to follow God and greet these others too, but finds it is difficult with hands tied to shake a hand or give a hug, etc.

Then Joyce moves to anxiety, which deals mostly with the future, and she ties up the same person's feet, just around the ankles. This person now has hands and feet tied simultaneously. Once again, someone playing God moves more quickly through the crowd, and this person tries to follow, often hopping or taking tiny quick steps, and sometimes falling. It is all very comical as you are watching it unfold, but the reality is that the truth of the matter can really sting because if you are one who is held and bound by regret or anxiety, it really is a problem for you. There is nothing funny about it at all.

The good news is that Jesus can and wants to set you free from these bondages that hinder you from running freely with Him. What is hindering you? Is it regret? Anxiety? What is holding you back from yielding to God?

Anxiety often portrays fears much larger than they should appear and comes up with all of the reasons why something won't work. It's almost a managerial response. Myles Munroe teaches that managers look at the bottom line (in other words, what it will cost), while CEOs and leaders look at the horizon. If you are a manager, Myles is not saying that all managers are bad, as the bottom line or cost is important. Jesus even addresses this situation in Luke 14:28 when those who were thinking of building a tower were reminded to count the cost in order to finish the building of that tower. But getting it on the drawing board to begin with takes a leader to see what a difference it will make on the horizon.

Our lives must be completed with the complementary tasks of seeing the bigger picture, but also with the intention of finishing the race. People often disqualify themselves by counting a cost that does not exist. Other times, the cost should have been counted to avoid costly mistakes. Then, there are those times we count the cost, and an obstacle still appears that we could not have possibly foreseen. But Jesus is still there to assist us. Even when a mistake is made, God can correct that mistake and cause things to turn out well. Romans 8:28 attests to that biblical truth: "And we know that all things work together for good to those who love God, to those who are the called according to His purpose."

One of the ways this happens is then given in verse 29 where we are told that we are to conform our lives to the image of Jesus Christ. This conformity often happens as we represent Him or re-present Him in each of life's situations and experiences. We become the earthly image of Jesus in our circumstances. Recently at a local church where I was ministering, I told this little story:

> There was a group of third graders drawing pictures in class one day. The teacher was walking around and admiring the pictures, complimenting the students and encouraging them in their art class. At one point, the teacher stopped by a young girl and asked what she was drawing, to which the little girl replied, "I am coloring a picture of God."
>
> The teacher responded, "Honey, no one knows what God looks like."
>
> But the little girl immediately answered and said, "They will when I am finished."

Do you want to see what God looks like? Go look in the mirror or take a glance at anyone you know who has a relationship with Jesus. You were created in His image, and you have His DNA. You are fearfully and wonderfully made. You are fantastic. And you look amazing! If you think otherwise, then you are questioning God's handiwork, and I certainly would encourage you not to indicate in any way that God may have made a mistake.

Sometimes the hindrance is so big that it automatically stops many from finishing. We saw that this year with the Boston Marathon, when just shortly after the bombs exploded the race officials called it off for those who were still blocks and in some cases miles away from finishing. Our race is in the kingdom, and Jesus is the official. He has given every one of us a chance to finish strong and not to be hindered by anything, including regret of the past and/or anxiety about the future. Even if faced with an opportunity to be tempted, He provides a way of escape there too. God has it covered for us.

I really like Galatians 5:1, which says, "Stand fast therefore in the liberty by which Christ has made us free, and do not be entangled again with a yoke of bondage." Isaiah 10:27 tells us that the anointing destroys the yoke. Jesus tells us in Matthew 11:29 to take on His yoke. Most of us know these verses but we don't appropriate them. People have a hard time appropriating forgiveness. They keep thinking of all the bad stuff they did and the likelihood that they may do it again. They center in the realm of regret and anxiety and thus stay entangled with that yoke of bondage. Most people who are in prison look forward to the day they will be set free and can walk out of prison. God says to stand in the liberty of freedom and not to go back to prison.

Isaiah 52:2 declares, "Shake yourself from the dust, arise; sit down, O Jerusalem! Loose yourself from the bonds of your neck, O captive daughter of Zion!" Zion is a picture of the church, and the daughter refers to the children of the Lord. Simply stated, there are some things that hold us in bondage that we can and must walk away from. We have the power and authority to loose ourselves from these things.

We can untie our hands bound in regret and loose our legs that are tied up in anxiety. Philippians 4:6–7 shares with us a simple yet profound way for this to be accomplished: "Be anxious for nothing, but in everything by prayer and supplication, with thanksgiving, let your requests be made known to God; and the peace of God, which surpasses all understanding, will guard your hearts and minds through Christ Jesus."

The Holy Spirit speaks to us through the Apostle Paul and simply reminds us to accomplish these things using various manners and models of prayer and His peace. I said, "And His peace." Paul said that the peace of God will guard and protect your heart and mind. Is that something you need right now? Let's just have a Selah Moment, which simply means to pause and reflect. We want to move away from *regret* to *reflect*.

To reflect means to think seriously about something. So, stop right now and reflect on what you have read thus far in this chapter. Simply approach God with your request in prayer and thanksgiving, and ask for His peace to come into you and upon you right now.

* * *

Did you pause and pray just now? I intentionally slowed the pace here, allowing you to stop, pause, and reflect. But the word *reflect* also means to give back or cast back an image like in a mirror. Now that the peace of God is working in your life, the peace of Jesus is reflecting a new image in you. It's similar to that passage above where I wrote about being created in the image of Jesus.

Bill Johnson clearly identifies this in the Gospel story where Jesus is asleep in the stern of the boat while there is a huge storm developing and the disciples are so fearful. Jesus awakens, and He calms the seas and the wind. Bill says that Jesus used peace to calm the storm and also used that same peace to sleep through the storm. Bill goes on to articulate that we really only have peace in storms that we can sleep through.[19]

Years ago, I was invited to Lake Charles, Louisiana, to minister at a Vineyard church there, and I was staying with the pastor at his home. This home had one of those sweeping staircases that had two points of origin at the bottom similar to what you might see in a Southern homes picture book. The home had bedrooms on either side of the upstairs, and mine was on the right as you faced the stairway from the bottom.

In the middle of the night, there was a rather intense storm that also spawned a tornado that ripped through the sugar cane fields, cutting pine trees in half and tearing into the other side of this house. It also broke windows and caused roof damage and some flooding downstairs. Believe it or not, I slept through the entire storm. Only after everyone was up in the house, moving about with flashlights because the power was off, did someone finally remember that I was up there on the other side of the house. Suddenly, they all rushed up to check on me, only to discover that I was sound asleep, safe in my room on my side of the house. Jesus had provided peace for me in the midst of that terrible storm. In the morning, when I saw the damage to the surrounding trees, farmer's fields, and other houses, I was simply amazed. It was clearly the hand of God in my life protecting me from that storm.

If you are in a storm right now, I want you to know that Jesus can and wants to protect you. Call upon Him and ask Him to help you stay and be at peace during this storm. Don't delay. Hebrews 4:16 says it this way: "Let us therefore come boldly to the throne of grace, that we may obtain mercy and find grace to help in time of need." Someone once asked, when faced with a crisis or a major problem, do you run to the phone or to the throne? People often run to the phone and talk to everyone but God. Jesus challenges us to run to His throne in any time of need.

This book has been all about yielding to God, plus seeing and discovering how yielding will then bring a yield back into our lives. It starts with the simple things in your life and mine. We don't jump to some of these larger things without first walking through some of the more mundane challenges in our lives. Jeremiah 17:7–8 give us this special message: "Blessed is the man who trusts in the Lord, and whose hope is the Lord. For he shall be like a tree planted by the waters, which spreads out its roots by the river, and will not fear when heat comes; but its leaf will be green, and will not be anxious in the year of drought, nor will cease from yielding fruit." The heat may be on in your life, but you can choose to trust God anyway, even when it makes no sense in the natural.

God desires that we simply trust Him and keep our hope centered on Him, making Him our entire aim. The returning promise to us is that even when things get tough, we will not cease from yielding fruit. How wonderful and amazing is that? I am thrilled to discover and share this spontaneous verse with you that was not in my notes, yet is perfectly applicable as we begin to conclude this chapter and this book.

What a phenomenal blessing! Or is it a benediction (a good word)? Oh, yeah, it is a good word, alright—so good that I can't stop writing about it right now. Here it is again.

> Blessed is the man who trusts in the Lord, and whose hope is the Lord. For he shall be like a tree planted by the waters, which spreads out its roots by the river, and will not fear when heat comes; but its leaf

will be green, and will not be anxious in the year of drought, nor will cease from yielding fruit.

Psalm 1:3 adds that these trees bring forth fruit in every season and shall always prosper. So if you're in the midst of a tough season, you can anticipate still bearing fruit.

Galatians 2:4–5 has another awesome promise and challenge associated with it. Watch for it as you read: "And this occurred because of false brethren secretly brought in (who came in by stealth to spy out our liberty which we have in Christ Jesus, that they might bring us into bondage), to whom we did not yield submission even for an hour, that the truth of the gospel might continue with you."

While speaking of a religious tradition, Paul just lays it on the line that the Galatian Christians did not yield to something that God was not calling them to, that the truth of the Gospel might continue. Again, this takes us back to Galatians 5:7, where the question is asked: Even though you used to run well, what has hindered you from obeying the truth? This theme seems to be recurring over and over in Galatians, as Paul is demonstrating to the church of that day and our day that the race for the kingdom and with Jesus is worth the cost, the fight, and the effort in every stage from the preparation to the race itself to finally finishing. Finish strong, my friend. Finish Strong!

I like what Psalm 85 says in these three verses: "Truth shall spring out of the earth, and righteousness shall look down from heaven. Yes, the LORD will give what is good; and our land will yield its increase. Righteousness will go before Him, and shall make His footsteps our path." Proverbs 4:26 tells us to ponder the path of our feet.

What path are you on? Where are you going? What are your intentions, now that you are about to finish this book? Where are you headed? What is God telling you? What wisdom or leading are you expecting from the Lord? My friend Jim used to say, "What's the deal, pickle?" (Dill pickle). Okay maybe not that one, but the rest are legitimate questions that you should consider answering.

God has something special for you to do, regardless of your age. I don't care how old you are. Psalm 92:14 says that the righteous shall still bear fruit in their old age. If you are still alive, then I believe He has a plan for you, with something significant for you to accomplish. Keep in mind that someday is not a day of the week. John Maxwell says that one of these days usually means none of these days. He also is quoted as stating that you don't have to be great to start but you do have to start to be great.

The Bible tells us that in order to be great in God's kingdom, we need to be the servant of others. Why not just start by serving God? He will then show you how to serve others simply by doing what you see Jesus doing. Yield to the Lord, and it will amaze you what will happen in the process. God's ways are perfect, and His knowledge of every situation is complete. His wisdom will fill every void with truth, love, and the kingdom way. Take Him at His Word and trust Him. Trust is a must!

Remember, James 3:17 says that the wisdom that is from above is first willing to yield.

Journey

You made it. This is a big book, and you made it through. I am proud of you. But if it is just another book that does not influence you to do something different or to be more radical for the kingdom of God, getting hot for God in a new on-fire kind of way, then I have failed as an author. We don't need more books that lack influence. What we need are anointed messages that motivate people to be filled with power and authority to go out like the disciples did and turn the world upside down. We don't want a subculture, but rather a counterculture. Will you help drive it?

I encourage you to pray to the Lord and ask for five objectives or vision statements that only God can give you. Write those down on the very next page or in your notebook, and then begin to ask God to unfold a plan and a strategy to accomplish these things. As He downloads this advice to you, simply begin to yield to Him and watch what He does. It will be life changing if you do. The other option is that this book, along with many others, will just start to collect dust like some of the other books on your shelves.

The book can collect dust, or you can inspire something that will leave the enemy in the dust behind what God is doing. You can begin to create your own whirlwind dust storm with heavenly energy that blows the wind of the Spirit into realms that up to this time have remained dry, brittle, and perhaps appear to be dying. But now, with God's Word etched in your heart and His power enabling you as you yield to Him, watch and see His yield come back to you in greater measure, with greater kingdom jurisdiction and more influence than you ever thought possible.

Begin to charge the gates of hell. Jesus told His disciples that the gates of hell would not prevail against His church. His intention was that every believer would charge the gates of hell and snatch more people out of the grasp of the enemy. Gates are defensive weapons, and they only function correctly if no one approaches them. God wants us to charge the gates, push back the enemy, and advance the kingdom of God in our spheres of influence. When you are running toward the gates, don't let anything hinder you in the process. You can continue to run well and with freedom.

We need captains who are launching spiritual warships, not harboring spiritual cruise lines. I hope that this book launches something in you that is so amazingly awesome that initially you can't even use words to describe it. I believe that whatever it is will ignite kingdom expansion while casting shadows of godly light on you and everything you touch.

I pray that God's favor rests on you in unfathomable ways as you proceed with God's plan in your life. May you be anointed with a fresh anointing. I pray that you stay in God's presence and walk with authority, responding to His directions with precision and functionality that model true discipleship for you as you follow Christ. It's time to wield the yield.

Epilogue

THROUGHOUT this book you read many different testimonies written by me and by others whom I know. Revelation 19:10 tells us that the testimony of Jesus is the spirit of prophecy, so when we hear a testimony of how God has worked in fantastic ways in the life of someone else, we can then apply that testimony as a prophetic word for our lives too. Wouldn't it be cool if your testimony actually projected and propelled others along in their lives while accessing the power of God to overcome a difficult situation because they heard or read your testimony?

I want to give you that opportunity to participate in future books, so if you would send me your testimony of how God worked in your life, I might be able to use that testimony in future books. Please contact me first by email at **anointed2go@cox.net** or use my blog to leave your testimony in the reply section at **www.anointed2go.com**.

I am actively recruiting such testimonies for my next published book and hope to hear from you soon.

For His Kingdom,
Pastor Jay W. West

Notes

1. Binion, David and Nicole. "Keeper of the Door." Covenant Worship. 2009.
2. "Theophany." *Wikipedia*. Wikimedia Foundation, 14 May 2013. Web. 28 May 2013.
3. As stated by Larry Lea in a message he preached in Rockwall, Texas.
4. Ziglar, Zig, and Tom Ziglar. *Born to Win: Find Your Success Code*. Dallas: Ziglar Success, 2012. Print.
5. Phillips, Donald L. *Healing Broken Lives & Relationships: Helping People Become Healthy Spiritually and Emotionally*. Fairfax, VA: Xulon, 2002. 125. Print.
6. Haley, Alex. *Roots*. Garden City, NY: Doubleday, 1976. Print.
7. Beautiful Savior Lutheran Church Newsletter (La Vista, NE). *Connections* (n.d.): n. pag. Print.
8. Matthews, William. "Deep Cries Out." By William Matthews, Amanda Gilbertson, and Christiann Koepke. Rec. 2010. *Be Lifted High*. Bethel Music. Bethel Music Publishing, 2010. CD.
9. Vallotton, Kris. *Heavy Rain: Reforming the Church to Transform the World*. Ventura, CA: Regal, 2010. Print.
10. Smith, Ben, Christian Paschall, and Pat Barrett. "Father Will You Come." 2009.
11. Konzelman, Brian. "Joy Is the Flag." His Eye Music/Universal Music - Brentwood Benson Tunes. 1979.
12. Swindoll, Charles R. *The Finishing Touch: Becoming God's Masterpiece*. Dallas, TX: World Pub., 1994. Print.
13. Pitts, Michael. "When Heaven Touches Earth Conference, Day 1." Sermon. Eagle's Nest Worship Center, 13 June 2011, Omaha.
14. Sheets, Dutch. *Intercessory Prayer: How God Can Use Your Prayers to Move Heaven and Earth*. Ventura: Gospel Light, 1997. Print.
15. Smith, Chuck. *Charisma vs. Charismania*. Eugene, Or.: Harvest House, 1983. Print.
16. For a more detailed account of how and why God called us to Omaha from Dallas, you will need to secure a copy of my first book *Downloads from Heaven* for a fuller disclosure.
17. Phillips, Donald L. *Healing Broken Lives & Relationships: Helping People Become Healthy Spiritually and Emotionally*. Fairfax, VA: Xulon, 2002. 125. Print.
18. West, Jason B. "Run with Freedom." By Jason B. West. *Running Free*. Jason West. BMI Work # 15825310, 2012. CD.
19. Johnson, Bill. "Chapter 5: Praying Heaven Down." *When Heaven Invades Earth*. Shippensburg: Destiny Image Pub, 2010. 66. Print.

Other Products Available from Anointed 2 Go MdM

Books

Downloads from Heaven
By Jay West
Suggested donation: $10

Who Will Ascend?
By Jason West
Suggested donation: $10

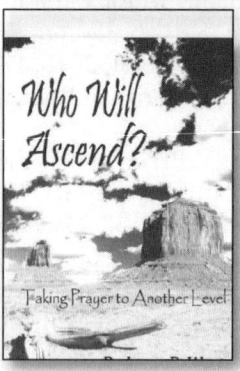

Worship CD

Running Free
Original songs by Jason West
Suggested donation: $10

Teaching DVD

"This Is a Great Day to Get Well"
By Jay West
Suggested donation: $10

Teaching CDs by Jay West

(Suggested donation: $5 each)

Being Uncommon in a Common World
Bypassing Religious Symbols and Hype
Challenging the Fears that Fearfully Challenge Us
Downloads from Heaven
Do You Need a Faith Lift?
Fresh Manna—Fresh Manifestation
Healing Power and Authority
Impartation for Healing
Peace—Gotta Have It
Shine Baby Shine
This Is a Great Day to Get Well
This Is Not My Recession
Waiting on God
Willing to Yield

To order these and other products from Anointed 2 Go, please contact:

Jay at **anointed2go@cox.net**

or

Jason at **runningfree@cox.net**

Please note that minimal shipping costs will be added to each order, which vary slightly with each order.